MW00479219

# The
# Official Rules of
# Inline Hockey

# The
# Official Rules of
# Inline Hockey

**BOOKS**

CHICAGO

Typographer: Sue Knopf
Illustrator: Mike Curti
Front cover photo courtesy of USA Hockey InLine

For more information on Inline and Ice Hockey, contact:

USA Hockey, Inc.
1775 Bob Johnson Drive
Colorado Springs, Colorado 80906
(719) 576-8724


This book is available in quantity at special discounts for your
group or organization. For more information, contact:

Triumph Books
601 South LaSalle Street
Suite 500
Chicago, Illinois 60605
Tel. (312) 939-3330 Fax (312) 663-3557

Printed in the United States of America

# User's Guide

The USA Hockey InLine Playing Rules have been designed to include both administrative and conduct rules.

Typically, administrative rules are those dealing with the setup and preparation of the game. Length of halves, size of arena, officiating systems and overtime regulations are examples of administrative rules.

Conduct rules pertain to the actual playing of the game. Rules regarding the scoring of goals, prescribed penalties for infractions, improper misconduct and mandatory equipment are examples of conduct rules.

Administrative rules may be changed only with permission from USA Hockey InLine that is obtained through the league sanctioning process.

Conduct rules may only be changed through the annual rules change process.

The Playing Rules contained in this publication are the official playing rules for all USA Hockey InLine State, Regional and National Championships.

USA Hockey InLine highly recommends that leagues utilize all playing rules in this publication to establish consistency throughout the sport of inline hockey, regardless of where it may be played.

Please note that the highlighted text within this edition of the Rule Book signifies an adjustment within that particular text.

This version of the Official Playing Rules will be considered the "official" playing rules of USA Hockey InLine through May 31, 2001.

# Contents

# Rules at a Glance

## PLAYING RULES AT A GLANCE

| Age Divisions | Boys'/Men's | Girls'/Women's |
|---|---|---|
| Mites | 8-and-Under | N/A |
| Squirts | 10-and-Under | 8-12 |
| Pee Wees | 12-and-Under | 13-15 |
| Bantams | 14-and-Under | N/A |
| Midgets | 17-and-Under | 16-19 |
| High School | Enrolled in High School | |
| Adults | 18-and-Over | Any Age |
| College/Club | Enrolled in College | |

*(Note 1) Girls/Women playing on a Boys'/Men's team must conform to the Boys'/ Men's age division.*

*(Note 2) To promote the standardization and consistency of the playing rules between leagues nationwide, sanctioned leagues must utilize the following age determination date(s):*

> *1999-2000 Membership Registration Season - Player's age on December 31, 1999*

> *2000-2001 Membership Registration Season - Player's age on December 31, 2000*

*(Note 3) The USA Hockey InLine Regional and National Championships will utilize the following age determination date(s) for the 1999, 2000 and 2001 Championships:*

> *1999 Regional and National Championships - Player's age on December 31, 1998*

---

> *2000 Regional and National Championships -*
> *Player's age on December 31, 1999*
>
> *2001 Regional and National Championships -*
> *Player's age on December 31, 2000*

*(Note 4) Leagues shall have the option of allowing*
*players to play up one age division, provided such a*
*player's skill level and physical maturity is of simi-*
*larity to other participants in the age division.*
*Allowing players to play down an age division is*
*prohibited.*

**Rule     Description**

**Rink**    Size is 145-185 feet long and 65-85 feet wide.
Temporary and permanent both acceptable.

**Teams**  4 players on playing surface plus 1 goalkeeper
(smaller rinks may play with 3 players plus 1
goalkeeper).

**Roster**  Maximum of 15 players plus 2 goalkeepers.

**Mandatory Equipment**

*Players 17-and-Under*

Helmet designed for hockey

Full face mask designed for hockey

Internal mouth guard

Elbow pads

Gloves designed for hockey or lacrosse

Knee and shin protection

---

*Players 18-and-Over*

Same, except no facial protection or internal mouthguard required. Wearing a full face mask or ½ face shield and internal mouthguard is highly recommended.

**Puck/Ball** Puck or Ball may be used. Puck may be used only when rink has boards that are 40 inches or more in height and adequate spectator screen protection. Regional and National Championships shall be played with a puck.

**Major Penalties** Carry an automatic game misconduct penalty to the offending player.

**Minor Penalties** Team cannot be reduced to less than two players plus a goalkeeper.

**Game Misconduct Penalties** Carry an automatic 1-game suspension.

**Referees** Standard two man system using current USA Hockey InLine registered officials.

**Body-Checking** No intentional body contact allowed at any level.

**Face-Offs** Take place at face-off spots only.

**Fighting** Fighting will not be tolerated. Major plus a Game Misconduct plus 1-game suspension.

**Hand Pass to a Teammate** Permitted in Defending Zone.

**Slapshots** Prohibited in 10-and-Under age groups and below (when back swing is higher than waist).

**Illegal Clearing (Icing)** No such rule.

**Off-Sides** No such rule. Passes may be made to a team-mate on the rink.

**Player Out of Bounds** Minor penalty for intentionally jumping out of bounds, unless doing so to avoid an injury (temporary rinks only).

**Length of Game** 2 halves, 15-25 minutes in duration each (Running time or stop time). If running time is played: Stoppage of play in the last two minutes when score is within 1 goal.

**Tied Game** Games shall end in a tie if no winner must be determined. If a winner must be determined: 5-minute overtime period followed by a shoot-out.

**Time-out** Each team is permitted 1 one-minute time-out per game. The game clock shall stop during a time-out.

# Rules Governing the Game of Inline Hockey

## SECTION ONE

## The Rink

## Rule 101 Rink

(a) The game of "inline hockey" shall be played on wood, cement, asphalt or plastic surface known as a "RINK."

(b) The rink may be an outdoor, partially enclosed or indoor facility.

## Rule 102 Dimensions of Rink

(a) As nearly as possible, the dimensions of the rink shall be 185 feet long and 85 feet wide. The minimum size for a rink shall be 145 feet long and 65 feet wide. In all rinks used for State, Regional and National Championships, the surface dimensions shall not be less than 165 feet long and 65 feet wide. It is recommended that the corners be uniformly rounded in the arc of a circle with a minimum radius of 20 feet and a maximum radius of 28 feet.

(b) The rink shall be surrounded by a permanent or temporary wall or fence known as the "BOARDS," which shall extend not less than 8 inches and not more than 48 inches in height above playing surface. The ideal height of the boards shall be 42 inches. It is recommended that the kick plate at the bottom of the boards be yellow or light in color.

    The boards shall be constructed in such a manner that the surface facing the playing surface shall be smooth and free of any obstruction or objects that could cause injury to players. All doors giving access to the playing surface must swing away from the playing surface.

It is recommended that each rink should include an equipment gate for emergency situations.

It is highly recommended that the entire rink, including players' and penalty benches, be enclosed with safety glass, fencing and/or other protective screens designed to separate players from spectators. All gear used to hold such equipment in place shall be mounted on the boards on the side away from the playing surface.

### Rule 103 | Goal Posts and Nets

(a) The goal frame shall be made of metal or other approved material. The goal posts shall be set 6 feet apart from the inside of the posts and the crossbar shall extend vertically 4 feet above the playing surface, connecting the tops of the goal posts. Alternative sizes are acceptable for regular house league play.

The goal posts and cross bar shall be painted red and all other exterior surfaces shall be painted white.

(b) Attached to each goal frame shall be netting strong enough to withstand any shot by a puck or ball.

(c) A minimum of 12 feet to a maximum of 15 feet from each end of the rink a red line 2 inches wide known as the "GOAL LINE" shall be painted extending completely across the rink and continuing vertically up the side boards.

The goal shall be centered on the goal line and shall be fixed in such a manner as to remain stationary during the progress of the game. The goal posts shall be anchored in such a manner as to permit a goal post to become dislodged when hit by a player with a significant degree of force.

Play shall be stopped immediately when the goal post has been displaced from its normal position.

## Rule 104 Goal Crease and Goalkeeper's Privileged Area

(a) In front of each goal, a "GOAL CREASE" shall be marked by a line 2 inches wide. The goal crease shall be laid out as follows: A semicircle 6 feet in radius and 2 inches in width shall be drawn using the center of the goal line as the center point.

In addition, an "L" shaped marking of 5 inches in length (both sides) at each front corner shall be painted on the surface. The location of the "L" marking is measured by drawing an imaginary line 4 inches from the goal line to the edge of the semicircle. At that point, the "L" shall be drawn.

(b) The goal crease area shall include all the space outlined by the semi-circular crease lines (including goal crease lines) and extending vertically four feet to the bottom of the cross bar.

(c) The goalkeeper's "PRIVILEGED AREA" is an area bounded in the rear by the end boards, in front by an imaginary line connecting the end zone face-off spots and on the sides by imaginary lines extending perpendicular from the end boards to the end zone face-off spots.

## Rule 105    Division of Playing Surface

(a)    The playing surface shall be divided into two
halves by a "CENTER RED LINE" 12 inches wide,
extending completely across the rink and continuing vertically up the side boards.

(b)    The center red line shall be considered to be a part
of the zone in which the puck/ball is located.

(c)    The half of the playing surface in which the goal is
situated shall be called the "DEFENDING ZONE"
of the team defending that goal. The half of the
playing surface furthest from the defending goal
shall be known as the "ATTACKING ZONE."

## Rule 106    Center Face-Off Spot and Circle

(a)    One 12-inch in diameter blue face-off spot shall be
at the exact center of the rink.
     With this spot as a center, a 15-foot radius cir-
cle shall be marked with a blue line 2 inches wide.
On both sides of the circle there shall be two lines
2 feet long, 2 inches wide and 4 feet apart.

## Rule 107    High Zone Face-Off Spots and Circles

(a)    Four red face-off spots 2 feet in diameter shall be
marked on the surface 18 feet from the center red
line along an imaginary line connecting the end
face-off spots. Within each face-off spot draw two
parallel lines 4 inches from the top and bottom of
the spot. The area within the two lines shall be
painted red.

## Rule 108   End Zone Face-Off Spots and Circles

(a)   In both zones and on both sides of each goal, red face-off spots and circles shall be marked on the playing surface. The face-off spots shall be 2 feet in diameter. Within each face-off spot draw two parallel lines 4 inches from the top and bottom of the spot. The area within the two lines shall be painted red.

With this spot as a center, a 15-foot radius circle shall be marked with a red line 2 inches wide. On both sides of the circle there shall be two lines 2 feet long, 2 inches wide and 4 feet apart.

(b)   The End Zone face-off spots shall be located equidistant from the side boards and 20 feet from each goal line. It is recommended that there be a 44 foot distance between the End Zone face-off spots in the same zone.

## Rule 109   Player Benches

(a)   Each rink shall have seats or benches for the use of each team. Each player bench shall have accommodations for at least 10 people and shall be placed immediately alongside the playing surface, as near as possible to the center of the rink.

All doors opening to the playing surface shall swing away from the playing surface.

(b)   Only players in uniform and Team Officials (up to a maximum of four) shall be permitted to occupy the bench area.

(c)   During a game, Coaches, Managers, and Trainers are restricted to the length of the player benches.

(d)   The use of tobacco products on the players' bench, penalty bench, timekeeper area, or on the playing surface is prohibited. For the first offense, a minor penalty shall be assessed. Thereafter, a game misconduct penalty shall be assessed.

(e)   The use of alcohol and illegal drugs on the players' bench, penalty bench, timekeeper area or on the playing surface is prohibited. For a violation of this rule, a game misconduct penalty shall be assessed.

### Rule 110   Penalty Bench

(a)   Each rink must be provided with seats or benches to be used for the seating of a penalized player, the Game Timekeeper, and Official Scorer. The penalty bench must be separated from the players' benches, ideally on the opposite side of the rink.

(b)   On the playing surface immediately in front of the Penalty Timekeeper's seat there shall be marked in red a semicircle of 10 foot radius and 2 inches wide which shall be known as the Referees Crease.

### Rule 111   Signal and Timing Devices

(a)   Each rink shall be provided with some form of electrical clock for the purpose of keeping the spectators, players and Game Officials accurately informed as to all time elements at all stages of the game, including the time remaining to be played.

Timing devices for both game time and penalty time shall show time remaining to be played or served.

(b) Each rink shall be provided with a siren, or other suitable sound device to signify the end of playing time.

(c) Behind each goal, electric lights or similar devices shall be set up for the use of the Goal Judges. A red light or other signal shall signify the scoring of a goal.

# Rules Governing the Game of Inline Hockey

## SECTION TWO

## Teams

### Rule 201  Composition of Team

(a)   A team shall be composed of four players on the
       playing surface, plus a goalkeeper. A maximum of
       15 players plus no more than 2 goalkeepers shall
       be permitted on any one team roster. No player,
       except goalkeepers, shall be permitted to be listed
       on two different team rosters in the same league,
       in the same age division. No team shall be allowed
       to start a game with less than five players on the
       playing surface, however, a team shall be permit-
       ted to start with five players and no goalkeeper.
       Anytime a team has been reduced to less than
       three players, the game shall be declared a forfeit.

### Rule 202  Captain of Team

(a)   One Captain shall be appointed by each team and
       only the Captain shall have the privilege of dis-
       cussing with the Referee any matter relating to
       the interpretation of rules which may arise during
       the course of a game.

       The Captain shall wear the letter "C," approxi-
       mately 3 inches in height and in contrasting color,
       in a conspicuous position on the front of the jer-
       sey.

       If the Captain is not available due to injury or
       penalty, another player may be designated to act
       as Captain.

       A complaint about a penalty is not a "matter
       relating to the interpretation of rules" and a minor
       penalty shall be assessed to any Captain or other
       player making such a complaint.

(b)    The Referee and Official Scorer shall be advised
       prior to the start of the game, of the names of the
       Captains of each team and the designated alternates.

(c)    Any player, except a goalkeeper, shall be entitled
       to be identified as the Captain.
          No playing Coach or Manager shall be permit-
       ted to act as Captain.

(d)    Any Captain or player who comes off the players'
       bench and makes any protest or intervention with
       the Officials for any purpose shall be assessed a
       minor penalty for Abuse of Officials.

## Rule 203   Players in Uniform

(a)    At the beginning of each game the Manager or
       Coach of each team shall list names and numbers
       of the players and goalkeepers who shall be eligi-
       ble to play in the game. No change or addition to
       the roster shall be permitted once the game has
       commenced.

(b)    Each team shall be allowed one goalkeeper on the
       playing surface at one time. The goalkeeper may
       be removed and another "player" substituted.
       Such substitute shall not be permitted the privi-
       leges of the goalkeeper.

(c)    It is recommended that each team have on its
       bench a substitute goalkeeper who shall be fully
       dressed and equipped to play.
          When the substitute goalkeeper enters the
       game the position shall be taken without delay
       and no warm-up shall be permitted.

(d)    Except when all designated goalkeepers are inca-
pacitated, no player on the playing roster in that
game shall be permitted to wear the equipment of
the goalkeeper. If a team's goalkeeper(s) is unavail-
able to continue, the team must immediately
appoint a temporary goalkeeper or place an additional skater on the playing surface with none of
the goalkeeper's privileges. A goalkeeper may be
substituted for by another goalkeeper during play
with full goalkeeper's privileges.

### Rule 204  Playing Lineup

(a)    Upon the Referee's signal prior to the start of the
game and following any stoppage of play, the Visiting Team shall promptly place a lineup on the
playing surface ready to play and no substitution
shall be made from that time until play has
resumed. The Home Team may then make any
desired substitution which does not result in the
delay of the game.

   If there is any undue delay by either team in
changing lines, the Referee shall order the offending team(s) to take their positions immediately
and not permit line changes.

   When a substitution has been made under the
above rule, no additional substitution may be
made until play commences, except when a
penalty is assessed.

### Rule 205  Change of Players

(a)    Players may be changed at any time from the players' bench, provided that the player or players

leaving the playing surface are within 5 feet of the players' bench and out of the play before the change is made.

If, in the course of making a substitution, either player deliberately plays the puck/ball while the retiring player is still on the playing surface, the infraction "Too Many Players" shall be assessed.

If, in the course of a substitution, either player is accidentally struck with the puck/ball, the play shall not be stopped and no penalty shall be assessed.

(b) A goalkeeper may be substituted for by a player or goalkeeper at any time during play. The goalkeeper must be within 5 feet of the players' bench before the substitute may enter the playing surface.

For a violation of this rule there shall be no time penalty to the team making the premature substitution, but the ensuing face-off shall take place at the center face-off spot.

(c) A player serving a penalty on the penalty bench, who is to be changed after the penalty has been served, must proceed at once by way of the playing surface before any change can be made. For a violation of this rule, a bench minor penalty shall be assessed.

(d) During a stoppage of play a goalkeeper may not go to the players' bench without the permission of the Referee unless there is a substitution by another player or goalkeeper. When a substitution is made under this rule, the replaced goalkeeper shall not return to the playing surface until play resumes, except that immediate re-entry into the game shall be permitted when a penalty is assessed to either team.

For a violation of this rule, a bench minor penalty shall be assessed.

## Rule 206  Injured Players

(a) When a player, other than a goalkeeper, is injured or compelled to leave the playing surface during a game, the player may retire from the game and be replaced immediately by a substitute.

(b) Any goalkeeper who sustains an injury or becomes ill must be ready to resume play immediately or be replaced by a substitute goalkeeper. No additional time shall be allowed by the Referee for the purpose of enabling the injured or ill goalkeeper to resume the position. The substitute goalkeeper shall enter the game without delay and no warm-up shall be permitted.

The substitute goalkeeper shall be subject to the regular rules governing goalkeepers and shall be entitled to the same privileges.

(c) Any penalized player who has been injured, may proceed to the dressing room without going to penalty bench. The penalized team shall immediately put a substitute player on the penalty bench to serve the entire penalty. The penalized player who has been injured and has been replaced on the penalty bench is not eligible to play until the penalty time has expired.

(d)   When a player is injured and cannot continue play or go to the players' bench, play shall not be stopped until the injured player's team has secured possession of the puck/ball. If the player's team is in possession of the puck/ball at the time of injury, play shall be stopped immediately unless the team has a scoring opportunity.

In the case where it is obvious that a player has sustained a serious injury, play shall be stopped immediately.

(e)   A player, other than the goalkeeper, whose injury appears serious enough to warrant a stoppage of play, may not participate further in the game until the completion of the ensuing face-off.

(f)   If a player or goalkeeper is obviously bleeding, play shall be stopped immediately and the injured player shall be ruled off the playing surface. Such player shall not be permitted to return to play until the bleeding has been stopped and the cut or abrasion covered.

Likewise, any Official who is bleeding shall not continue until the bleeding has been stopped and the cut or abrasion covered.

# Rules Governing the Game of Inline Hockey

## SECTION THREE

## Equipment

## Rule 301 Sticks

(a)　The sticks shall be made of wood, carbon composite, graphite or aluminum materials approved by USA Hockey InLine and must not have any projections extending from the stick.

　　Adhesive tape of any color may be wrapped around the stick at any place.

(b)　No stick shall exceed 60 inches in length from the heel to the end of the shaft, nor more than 12½ inches from the heel to the end of the blade.

　　The blade of the stick shall not be less than 2 inches nor more than 3 inches in width at any point.

　　The curvature of the blade of the stick shall not be restricted. It is recommended, however, that the curvature of the blade of the stick not exceed ½ inch.

(c)　The blade of the goalkeeper's stick shall not exceed 3½ inches in width at any point except at the heel where it shall not exceed 4½ inches. The length of the blade shall not exceed 15½ inches in length from the heel to the end of the blade.

　　The widened portion of the goalkeeper's stick extending up the shaft from the blade shall not extend more than 26 inches from the heel and shall not exceed 3½ inches in width.

(d)　A minor penalty shall be assessed to any player or goalkeeper who uses a stick not conforming to the provisions of this rule.

　　If a goal is scored with an illegal stick, the

proper penalty shall be assessed and the goal shall be allowed.

(e) A minor penalty shall be assessed to a player or goalkeeper who participates in the play while in possession of more than one stick, except that no penalty shall be assessed to a player who is accidentally struck by the puck/ball while carrying a replacement stick to a teammate.

## Rule 302  Skates

(a) All players and officials should wear skates designed for inline hockey with a maximum of five wheels. Brakes are optional.

(b) The use of speed skates or any skate so designed that it may cause injury is prohibited. The use of quad skates is not prohibited, but is not recommended.

## Rule 303  Goalkeeper's Equipment

(a) With the exception of skates and stick, all the equipment worn by the goalkeeper must be constructed solely for the protection of the head or body, and must not include any garment or contrivance which would give the goalkeeper undue assistance in keeping goal.

Abdominal aprons extending down the thighs or the outside of the pants are prohibited.

(b) The goalkeeper's blocker glove shall not exceed 8 inches in width nor 16 inches in length at any point.

The maximum length of a goalkeeper's catching glove shall not exceed 17 inches. The cuff shall not exceed 9 inches in width. Any bar or attachment between the cuff and the thumb shall only extend in a straight line. Any other pocket or pouch added to the glove by a manufacturer or otherwise is not acceptable and makes the glove illegal.

For a violation of this rule, a minor penalty shall be assessed.

(c) The leg guards worn by goalkeepers shall not exceed 12 inches in extreme width when on the leg of the player.

For a violation of this rule, a minor penalty shall be assessed.

(d) It is mandatory for all goalkeepers to wear a helmet designed for hockey with helmet strap properly fastened and a full face mask designed for hockey with a chin cup. All goalkeepers must wear chest protection. Throat protection is recommended.

## Rule 304 Protective Equipment

*(Note) Although some protective equipment is not mandatory in all age divisions, USA Hockey InLine strongly recommends that all players in all age divisions properly wear an internal mouthpiece, a H.E.C.C. approved helmet and a H.E.C.C. approved full face mask for all games and practices.*

(a)  Each participant is personally responsible to wear protective equipment for all games, warm-ups and practices.

Recommended equipment for all players is: hip pads, padded hockey pants, protective cup or pelvic protector, chest protection, shoulder pads and throat protection. Eye and full facial protection is strongly recommended for players 18 years and older in the 18-and-over age division.

Mandatory equipment for the High School age division and below includes: helmet designed for hockey with helmet strap properly fastened, full face mask designed for hockey with a chin cup, colored (non-clear) internal mouth guard, elbow pads, gloves designed for hockey, and knee and shin protection designed for hockey.

Mandatory equipment for the 18-and-over age division includes: helmet designed for hockey with helmet strap properly fastened, elbow pads, gloves designed for hockey, and knee and shin protection designed for hockey, in addition, for players under 18 years of age, a colored (non-clear) internal mouth guard and full facemask designed for hockey with chin cup are required.

All Referees and Linesmen must wear a black helmet designed for hockey with helmet strap properly fastened, elbow pads and knee and shin protection.

If an injury occurs while a player is not wearing any of the above mentioned mandatory equipment, the insurance carrier may not be responsible for the claim.

Any player who attempts to participate without the proper mandatory equipment shall be sent off the playing surface by the Referee and not allowed to return until such equipment has been replaced. For a second violation of this rule by the same player, the Referee shall assess a misconduct penalty to the offending player.

(b) It is recommended that all protective equipment, except gloves, head gear and goalkeeper leg pads, be entirely under the uniform.

(c) A player, other than a goalkeeper, whose helmet/face mask has come off the head during play may not resume play until it has been replaced. For a violation of this rule, a minor penalty shall be assessed. If the goalkeeper's helmet/face mask comes off during play, the play shall be stopped immediately. A minor penalty shall be assessed to a goalkeeper who deliberately removes the helmet/face mask during play.

(d) Players on the players' and penalty bench must wear the protective helmet/face mask while in the bench area. For a violation of this rule, a misconduct penalty shall be assessed to the offending player.

### Rule 305 Dangerous Equipment

(a) The use of pads or protectors made of metal or any other material that may cause injury to a player is prohibited.

The wearing of casts or splints made of hard or unyielding materials is prohibited, even if padded.

Elbow pads which do not have a soft protective covering of sponge rubber or a similar material at least ½ inch thick shall be considered dangerous equipment.

(b) A glove from which all or part of the palm has been removed or cut to permit the use of the bare hand shall be considered illegal equipment. A minor penalty shall be assessed to a player wearing such a glove in play.

(c) The wearing of jewelry that is visible to the referee is prohibited and any offending player shall be sent off the playing surface until the jewelry is removed.

(d) The wearing of casts or splints made of hard or unyielding materials is prohibited, unless directed in writing by a licensed medical physician. Such casts or splints must be covered on all exterior surfaces with no less then ½-inch thick, high density, closed cell polyurethane or alternate material of the same minimum thickness and similar physical properties, to protect opponents from injury.

## Rule 306 Puck/Ball

(a) Pucks/balls shall be made of plastic or other material approved by USA Hockey InLine. Balls should be classified as "no bounce" balls.

The puck shall be approximately 1 inch thick, and 3 inches in diameter and shall weigh between 3½ and 6½ ounces.

The ball shall be between 2½ inches and 2¾

inches in diameter and shall weigh between 1.75 and 3 ounces.

(b) The puck/ball shall be of a predominant color that contrasts with the color of the playing surface.

(c) On all rinks which have boards less than 40 inches in height and/or no screens for protection of the spectators, a ball must be used.

Pucks may be used on rinks that have boards at least 40 inches in height and screens or safety glass for protection of the spectators.

For all State, Regional and National Championships, a puck shall be used.

## Rule 307 Uniforms

(a) All players participating in USA Hockey InLine games must be uniformly dressed and have matching jerseys with long sleeves. For all State, Regional and National Championships, players must wear a uniform that covers all protective equipment except skates, gloves and helmet/face-masks.

(b) Each player and each goalkeeper listed in the lineup must wear an individual identifying number at least 8 inches in height on the back of the sweater. All numbers assigned must be whole numbers between 0-99. No two members of the same team shall be permitted to wear the same number.

(c) At the discretion of the Referee, the Home Team shall change its jerseys if the colors of the competing teams conflict.

## Rule 308 Equipment Measurement

(a)   A request for measurement of any equipment shall
be limited to one request by each team during the
course of any stoppage of play.

(b)   When a formal complaint is made by the Captain
of a team against the dimensions of any stick, the
Referee shall make the necessary measurement
immediately. If the complaint is not sustained, a
bench minor penalty shall be assessed to the team
requesting the measurement.

    When a formal complaint is made by the Cap-
tain of a team against the dimensions of any piece
of goalkeeper's equipment and the measurement
would cause any delay whatsoever, other than
glove measurement, such measurement shall take
place at the end of the first half or immediately in
the second half or overtime. If the complaint is
not sustained, a bench minor penalty shall be
assessed to the team requesting the measurement.

(c)   A minor plus a misconduct penalty shall be
assessed to any player who refuses to surrender
the stick or other piece of equipment for measurement when requested to do so by the Referee.

(d)   The Referee may measure any equipment used for
the first time in the game.

(e)   The Referee shall assess a bench minor penalty to
a team that requests a measurement of equipment
only for the purpose of delaying the game.

# Rules Governing the Game of Inline Hockey

## SECTION FOUR

## Penalties

## Rule 401 Penalties

(a)  Penalties shall be actual playing time and shall be divided into the following classes:

1. Minor Penalties

2. Bench Minor Penalties

3. Major Penalties

4. Misconduct Penalties

5. Match Penalties

6. Penalty Shot

(b)  When play is not actually in progress and an offense is committed by any player or Team Official, the same penalty shall apply as though play were actually in progress.

## Rule 402 Minor Penalties

(a)  For a "MINOR PENALTY," any player, other than a goalkeeper, shall be ruled off the playing surface for two minutes, during which time no substitute shall be permitted.

    When running time is being played, the penalty will start at the moment the ensuing face-off is conducted. If a minor or bench minor penalty terminates during a stoppage of play, allowing the team to have an additional player on the playing surface, the player so penalized shall remain on the penalty bench until the ensuing face-off is conducted.

(b)    For a "BENCH MINOR PENALTY" one player of
the penalized team shall be ruled off the playing
surface for two minutes, during which time no
substitute shall be permitted. Any non-penalized
player, other than a goalkeeper, may be designated
to serve the penalty by the Coach or Manager and
such player shall immediately serve the penalty.

(c)    If the opposing team scores a goal while a team is
shorthanded by one or more minor or bench minor
penalties, the first of such penalties shall automatically terminate.

"Shorthanded" means that the team must be
below the numerical strength of its opponents on
the playing surface at the time the goal is scored.
Thus, if an equal number of players from each
team are serving an equal number of minor penalties, neither team is "shorthanded."

This rule shall also apply when a goal is scored
on a penalty shot or an awarded goal.

(d)    When the minor penalties of two players of the
same team terminate at the same time, the Captain of that team shall designate to the Referee
which player shall return to the playing surface
first and the Referee shall instruct the Penalty
Timekeeper accordingly.

(e)    When a player receives a major penalty and a
minor penalty at the same time, the major penalty
shall be served first by the penalized player except
if the major penalties are coincident, in which
case the minor penalty shall be served first.

(f) When coincident minor penalties are assessed to players of both teams, the penalized players shall take their place on the penalty bench and such players shall not leave the penalty bench until the first stoppage of play following the expiration on their respective penalties. Immediate substitutions shall be made for an equal number of minor penalties or coincident minor penalties of equal duration to each team so penalized and the penalties of the players for whom substitutions have been made shall not be taken into account for the purpose of a delayed penalty.

## Rule 403  Major Penalties

(a) For a "MAJOR PENALTY," the offending player shall be assessed a game misconduct penalty and the offending team shall be short-handed for five minutes, during which time no substitute shall be permitted.

(b) When coincident major penalties or coincident penalties of equal duration including a major penalty are assessed to players of both teams, the offending team(s) shall place a substitute player(s) on the penalty bench and such penalized players shall not leave the penalty bench until the first stoppage of play following the expiration of their respective penalties.

   Immediate substitutions on the playing surface shall be made for an equal number of major penalties or coincident penalties of equal duration including a major penalty to each team so penal-

ized and the penalties of the players for which substitutions have been made shall not be taken into
account for the purpose of a delayed penalty.

Where it is required to determine which of the
penalized players shall be designated to serve the
delayed penalty under Rule 408, the penalized
team shall have the right to make such designa-
tion not in conflict with Rule 402.

(c) When coincident penalties of unequal duration
(each including one major penalty) are assessed to
one player of each team, the penalized players
shall be assessed a game misconduct penalty and a
substitute player shall serve any additional penalties other than the coincidental major penalty.

The penalties which create the disparity in
total penalty time shall be served first in the normal manner by the penalized players. Immediate
substitutions on the playing surface shall be permitted for the major penalties of each player.

## Rule 404  Misconduct Penalties

(a) A "MISCONDUCT PENALTY" involves the
removal of a player, other than a goalkeeper, for a
period of 10 minutes, but another player is permitted to immediately replace a player so removed. A
player whose misconduct penalty has expired shall
remain in the penalty bench until the next stoppage of play.

Unless immediate substitution is permitted
under coincident penalty rules 402 and 403, when
a player receives a minor or major penalty and a

misconduct, game misconduct or a gross misconduct penalty at the same time, the penalized team shall immediately place an additional non-penalized player, other than a goalkeeper, on the penalty bench and such player may not be changed.

Any violation of this provision shall be treated as illegal substitution under Rule 205.

(b) A "GAME MISCONDUCT" penalty involves the suspension of a player for the balance of the game, but a substitute is permitted to replace the player so removed.

(c) A player or Team Official incurring a game misconduct penalty to a player shall be suspended for the next game of that team.

The Referee is required to report all game misconduct penalties and all surrounding circumstances to the League Authorities immediately following the game. The League Authorities shall have full power to impose further penalties.

For all game misconduct penalties regardless of when assessed, a total of 10 minutes shall be charged in the records against the offending player.

(d) A "GROSS MISCONDUCT" penalty involves the suspension of a player or Team Official for the balance of the game, but another player is permitted to replace a player so removed.

The Referee is required to report all gross misconduct penalties and the surrounding circumstances to the League Authorities immediately following the game. The League Authorities shall have full power to impose further penalties.

For all gross misconduct penalties regardless of when assessed, a total of 10 minutes shall be charged in the records against the offending player.

(e)    A player who has been assessed a gross misconduct penalty shall be suspended from participating in any games or practices until the case has been dealt with by the League Authorities.

A mandatory hearing shall be held and a decision made relative to any further disciplinary action within 30 days of the incident. If circumstances prevent the League Authorities from conducting the hearing, the suspension shall be automatically terminated after 30 days.

It is recommended that league and tournament officials establish a disciplinary committee to conduct such hearings in an efficient and timely manner.

(f)    A Team Official who is assessed a game misconduct or a gross misconduct penalty, may not sit near the team bench, nor in any way attempt to direct the play of the team.

## Rule 405   Match Penalties

(a)    A "MATCH PENALTY" involves the suspension of a player for the balance of the game and the offending player shall be ordered to the dressing room immediately. Unless immediate substitution is permitted under the coincident penalty

rules 403 and 405, the penalized team shall immediately place a non-penalized player, other than a
goalkeeper, on the penalty bench to serve the five-
minute time portion of the penalty and such
player may not be changed.

The player shall also serve any additional minor
or major penalty assessed to the offending player
unless immediate substitution is permitted under
coincident penalty rules 402 and 403.

The Referee is required to report all match
penalties and all surrounding circumstances to the
League Authorities immediately following the
game. The League Authorities shall have full
power to impose further penalties.

For all match penalties, regardless of when
assessed, a total of 10 minutes shall be charged in
the records against the offending player.

(b) When coincident match penalties have been
assessed or when any combination of coincident
major and match penalties have been assessed to a
player or players of both teams, rule 403 covering
major penalties shall be applicable with respect to
player substitutions.

(c) A player who has been assessed a match penalty
shall be suspended from participating in any
games or practices until the case has been dealt
with by the League Authorities.

A mandatory hearing shall be held and a decision made relative to any further disciplinary
action within 30 days of the incident. If circumstances prevent the League Authorities from con-

ducting the hearing, the suspension shall be automatically terminated after 30 days.

It is recommended that league and tournament officials establish a disciplinary committee to conduct such hearings in an efficient and timely manner.

## Rule 406 Penalty Shot

(a) Any infraction of the rules which calls for a "Penalty Shot" shall be taken as follows:

The Referee shall identify the player entitled to take the shot (as appropriate) and shall then place the puck/ball on the center face-off spot. The player taking the shot shall, on the whistle of the Referee, play the puck/ball and shall attempt to score on the goalkeeper. Once the player taking the shot has touched the puck/ball, it must be kept in motion towards the opponent's goal line and once it is shot, the play shall be considered complete.

No goal can be scored on a rebound of any kind and any time the puck/ball crosses the goal line the shot shall be considered complete.

Only a player designated as a goalkeeper, substitute goalkeeper or temporary goalkeeper may defend against a penalty shot.

(b) The goalkeeper must remain in the goal crease until the Referee blows the whistle to start the penalty shot and the player taking the shot touches the puck/ball with their stick. In the event of violation of this rule or any foul committed by a goalkeeper the Referee shall allow the shot to be taken and if the shot fails the Referee shall permit the penalty shot to be taken again.

The goalkeeper may attempt to stop the shot in any manner except by throwing the stick or any other object, in which case a goal shall be awarded.

(c)  In cases where a penalty shot has been awarded under Rule 609 deliberately displacing goal post or removing helmet/facemask during a breakaway and under Rule 639 for fouling from behind, the Referee shall designate the player who has been fouled as the player who takes the penalty shot.

In cases where a penalty shot has been awarded under Rule 609 delaying the game, Rule 612 falling on the puck/ball in the goal crease, Rule 616 picking up the puck/ball from the goal crease area, Rule 625 illegal entry into the game, and Rule 636 for throwing a stick, the penalty shot shall be taken by a player selected by the Coach, or in the absence of the Coach, the Captain of the non-offending team from all non-penalized, non-injured players, excluding goalkeepers, on the team. Such selection shall be reported to the Referee and cannot be changed.

If by reason of injury the player designated by a Referee to take the penalty shot is unable to do so, the shot may be taken by a player selected by the Coach, or in the absence of the Coach, the Captain of the non-offending team from all non-penalized, non-injured players, excluding goalkeepers, on the team. Such selection shall be reported to the Referee and cannot be changed.

(d) Should the player in respect to whom a penalty shot has been awarded, commit a foul in connection with the same play or circumstances, either before or after the penalty shot has been awarded, the player shall be first permitted to take the shot before being sent to the penalty bench to serve the penalty, except when such a penalty is for a game misconduct, gross misconduct or match penalty in which case the penalty shot shall be taken by a player selected by the Coach, or in the absence of the Coach, the Captain of the non-offending team from all non-penalized, non-injured players, excluding goalkeepers, on the team.

If, at the time a penalty shot is awarded, the goalkeeper of the penalized team has been removed from the playing surface for another player, the goalkeeper shall be permitted to return to the playing surface before the penalty shot is taken.

(e) While the penalty shot is being taken, all players of both teams except those involved with the taking of the penalty shot, must withdraw from the playing surface onto their respective players' bench.

(f) If, while the penalty shot is being taken, any player of the opposing team shall interfere with or distract the player taking the shot, a goal shall be awarded.

(g)    If the goal is scored during a penalty shot, the
       puck/ball shall be faced-off at the center spot. If a
       goal is not scored, the puck/ball shall be faced-off
       at either of the end face-off spots in the zone in
       which the penalty shot was taken.

(h)    Whether or not a goal is scored from a penalty
       shot, if an infraction for which the penalty shot
       was awarded was such to incur:

       1. a major, match or misconduct penalty, the
          penalty shall be assessed in addition to the
          penalty shot.

       2. a minor or bench minor penalty, a further
          penalty to the offending player shall not be
          applied.

(i)    If the foul upon which the penalty shot is based
       occurs during actual playing time, the penalty
       shot shall be awarded and taken immediately fol-
       lowing the normal stoppage of play.
          The time required for the taking of a penalty
       shot shall not be included in the regular playing
       time.

## Rule 407 Goalkeeper Penalties

(a)    A goalkeeper shall not be sent to the penalty
       bench for an infraction which incurs a minor,
       major or misconduct penalty, but instead the
       penalty shall be served by a teammate who was on
       the playing surface at the time the infraction was
       committed. Such player shall be designated by the
       Coach and shall not be changed.

(b)  When a goalkeeper incurs a game misconduct penalty, the position shall be taken by a team-mate, or by a substitute or temporary goalkeeper who is available, and such player shall be allowed the goalkeeper's full equipment.

(c)  When a goalkeeper incurs a match penalty, the position shall be taken by a teammate or a substitute goalkeeper who is available, and such player shall be allowed the goalkeeper's equipment. However, any additional penalties specifically called for by the individual rules covering match penalties shall apply, and the offending team shall be penalized accordingly. Such additional penalty shall be served by another member of the team who was on the playing surface at the time the infraction was committed. Such player is to be designated by the Coach through the playing Captain and shall not be changed.

(d)  All penalties assessed to a goalkeeper, regardless of who serves the penalty, or any substitution, shall be charged in the records against the goalkeeper.

(e)  A minor penalty shall be assessed to a goalkeeper who participates in the play in any manner beyond the center line.

## Rule 408　Delayed Penalties

(a)  If a third player of any team is penalized while two players of the same team are serving penalties, the penalty time of the third player shall not commence until the penalty time of one of the two players already penalized has elapsed. Nevertheless, the third player penalized must immediately proceed to the penalty bench and may be replaced by a substitute until such time as the penalty time of the penalized player shall commence.

(b)     When any team shall have three players serving penalties at the same time and because of the delayed penalty rule a substitute for the third offender is in the playing surface, none of the three penalized players on the penalty bench may return to the playing surface until play has been stopped. When the play has been stopped, the player(s) whose full penalty has expired may return to the playing surface.

The Penalty Timekeeper shall permit the return to the playing surface in the order of expiration of their penalties, of a player or players when by reason of the expiration of their penalties the penalized team is entitled to have more than three players on the playing surface.

(c)     In the case of delayed penalties, the penalized players whose penalties have expired shall only be allowed to return to the playing surface when there is a stoppage of play.

When the penalties of two players of the same team shall expire at the same time, the Captain of that team shall designate to the Referee which player shall return to the playing surface first and the Referee shall instruct the Penalty Timekeeper accordingly.

When a major and a minor penalty are assessed at the same time to different players of the same team, the minor penalty shall be recorded as being the first of such penalties.

## Rule 409 Calling of Penalties

(a) Should an infraction of the rules be committed by a player of the team in possession of the puck/ball, the Referee shall immediately stop play and assess the penalty(s) to the offending player(s).

(b) Should an infraction of the rules which call for a minor, bench minor, major or match penalty, as committed by a player of a team not in possession of the puck/ball, the Referee shall signify the calling of a delayed penalty by raising the arm and, on completion of the play by the team in possession, shall immediately stop play and assess the penalty to the offending player.

"Completion of the play by the team in possession" in this rule means that the puck/ball must have come into the possession and control of an opposing player, or has been "frozen." This does not mean a rebound off the goalkeeper, the goal or the boards or any accidental contact with the body or equipment of an opposing player.

(c) The ensuing face-off shall take place at the face-off spot nearest to the location of the puck/ball when play is stopped unless the stoppage occurs in the Attacking Zone of the player penalized, in which case the face-off shall be conducted at the nearest high zone face-off spot.

(d) If the penalty to be assessed is a minor penalty, and a goal is scored on the play by the non-offending team, the minor penalty shall not be assessed, but all other minor, major or match penalties shall be assessed in the normal manner regardless of whether or not a goal is scored.

(e) If, after the Referee has signaled a penalty, but before play has been stopped, the puck/ball enters the goal of the non-offending team as the direct result of the action of a player of that team, the goal shall be allowed and the penalty signaled shall be assessed in the normal manner.

(f) If the Referee signals an additional minor penalty(s) against a team that is already short-handed because of one or more minor or bench minor penalties, and a goal is scored by the non-offending team before the whistle is blown, the goal shall be allowed, the delayed penalty(s) shall not be assessed and the minor penalty being served which caused the team to be shorthanded shall terminate automatically.

(g) Should the same offending player commit other fouls on the same play, either before or after the Referee has stopped play, the offending player shall serve such penalties consecutively.

(h) All minor and bench minor penalties occurring after a goal has been scored or during the stoppage of play when a penalty shot is being attempted, shall be served in the normal manner under this rule.

## Rule 410 Supplementary Discipline

(a) In addition to the suspensions assessed under these rules, the League Authorities may, at the conclusion of the game, at their discretion, investigate any incident that occurs in connection with any game and may assess additional suspensions for any offense committed before, during or after any game by a player or Team Official, whether or not such offense had been penalized by the Referee.

(b) Suspensions assessed during a USA Hockey InLine State, District or Regional Play-Off or National Championship, must be served during that same tournament. If the length of the suspension carries beyond that tournament for an advancing team, the Discipline Committee of the following tournament shall be the sole authority in determining the eligibility of the individual(s).

# Rules Governing the Game of Inline Hockey

## SECTION FIVE

## Officials

### Rule 501 **Appointment of Officials**

(a) Referee system- The official methods of officiating USA Hockey InLine games is with two Referees (2-man system) or with one Referee and two Linesmen (3-man system).

   When a 2-man system is utilized, the duties of the Linesmen under Rule 503 shall be carried out by both Referees, in addition to the duties of the Referee under Rule 502.

(b) Referees and Linesmen shall be controlled and assigned by the Inline League or by the Local Officials Association.

   For Regional Playoffs and National Championships, the District Referee-in-Chief or the duly appointed representative shall appoint all Referees and Linesmen.

(c) The Referee(s) and Linesmen shall have full authority and final decision in all matters of dispute, and not subject to appeal, during the course of the game.

(d) All Referees and Linesmen shall wear black trousers, black and white striped sweaters designed for hockey, a black hockey helmet with chin strap properly fastened, elbow pads and shin and knee protection.

   Referees and Linesmen shall wear the current USA Hockey InLine Officials crest on the left chest of the sweater during all games. Any other crest that is worn shall be placed on either arm of the sweater. The wearing of name plates shall be regulated by each league.

Referees shall be equipped with finger whistles and metal tape measures with a minimum length of 6 feet.

(e) For tournament play, the Tournament Committee shall appoint a Game Timekeeper, a Penalty Timekeeper, an Official Scorer and two Goal Judges.

## Rule 502 Referee

(a) The "REFEREE" shall have general supervision of the game and shall have full control of all Game Officials and players before, during and after the game, on and off the playing surface. In case of any dispute, the decision of the Referee shall be final.

The Referees shall enter the playing surface prior to warm-ups and remain on the surface at the conclusion of each half until all players have proceeded to their dressing rooms. Penalties may be assessed at any time before, during and after the game.

(b) Prior to each game, the Referee shall check the USA Hockey InLine member cards of each player and Coach against the game roster. Any participant who does not possess a card shall not be allowed to participate.

(c) The Referee shall order the teams onto the playing surface at the appointed time for the beginning of each game and at the start of each half.

If for any reason there should be more than fifteen minutes delay in the commencement of the game or any undue delay in resuming play for the second half, the Referee shall state in the report to the League Authorities the cause of the delay and the team(s) that was at fault.

(d) The Referee shall make a visual inspection of all players during the warm-up. If there is any lack of conformity to the regulations on mandatory equipment, the Referee shall ensure that the required equipment is in place.

(e) The Referee shall, prior to the start of the game, see that the appointed Game Timekeeper, Penalty Timekeeper, Official Scorer and Goal Judges are in their respective places and that the timing and signaling equipment is in good working order.

(f) The Referee shall impose such penalties as are prescribed by the rules for infractions thereof and the Referee shall have the final decision regarding all goals. The Referee shall consult with the Linesmen and the Goal Judge, if necessary, before making a final decision.

(g) The Referee shall report to the Official Scorer, or Penalty Timekeeper, all goals and assists legally scored and all penalties assessed and the reason for the assessment of such penalties.

The Referee shall report the reason for not allowing a goal every time the goal light is turned on in error during the course of play and every time a goal is illegally scored.

(h) If the Referees (2-man system) cannot appear for a game or are unable to continue due to illness or injury, the Managers or Coaches of the teams shall agree on Referee(s) and Linesmen. If they are unable to agree, they shall appoint a player from each team who shall act as Referee and Linesman. The player of the home team shall act as the Referee and the player of the visiting team shall act as the Linesman.

Should a Linesman (3-man system) be unable to appear or unable to continue due to illness or injury, the Referee shall have the power to appoint another, if deemed necessary or, if required to do so, by the Coach or Manager of either of the competing teams.

Should the Referee (3-man system) be unable to continue to officiate due to illness or injury, one of the Linesmen shall perform the duties of the Referee during the balance of the game. The Linesman shall be selected by the Referee or, if required to do so, by the Coaches or Managers of the competing teams.

If the regularly appointed Officials appear during the progress of the game, they shall at once replace the temporary Officials.

(i)  After each game, the Referees shall check and sign the score sheet and return it to the Official Scorer.

Referees are required to report to the League Authorities all game misconduct, gross misconduct and match penalties immediately following the game giving full details of the circumstances surrounding the incident.

## Rule 503 Linesmen

(a) The duties of the "LINESMEN" shall be to assist the Referee in the overall conduct of the game.

   The Linesman shall stop play when the puck/ball goes outside the playing area, when it is interfered with by any ineligible person, when it is struck above the height of the shoulder, when it is passed to a teammate with the hand and when the goal post has been displaced from its normal position. When in the vicinity of the goal, the Linesman shall stop play when the puck/ball is observed entering the goal. The Linesman shall stop play for off-sides occurring at the face-off circles and when there has been a premature substitution for a goalkeeper under Rule 205, for injured players under Rule 206 and for interference by spectators under Rule 622.

(b) The Linesman shall conduct face-offs at all times, except at the start of a half and after a goal has been scored.

(c) The Linesman shall, when requested to do so by the Referee, describe any incident that may have taken place during the playing of the game.

(d) The Linesman shall not stop play to assess any penalty except for any violation of too many players under Rule 205, articles thrown onto the playing surface under Rule 601 and illegally received replacement stick under Rule 605. The Linesman shall report such violations to the Referee who shall assess a bench minor penalty to the offending team.

The Linesman shall report immediately to the Referee the circumstances surrounding any violation of delaying the game under Rule 609 and any infraction of the rules which constitutes a bench minor, major, misconduct, game misconduct, gross misconduct, match penalty or penalty shot. The Referee may assess a penalty for such infractions.

(e) If the Referee accidentally leaves the playing area or receives an incapacitating injury, while play is in progress, the Linesman shall stop play immediately.

## Rule 504 Goal Judges

(a) There shall be one "GOAL JUDGE" at each end of the rink. They shall not be members of either team engaged in the game, nor shall they be replaced after the start of the game, unless it becomes apparent to the Referee that either Goal Judge makes unjust decisions, in which case, the Referee shall appoint a replacement.

(b) The Goal Judges shall be stationed behind the goals during the progress of the game in properly screened cages so there can be no interference with their activities. They shall not change goals during the game.

(c) In the event of a goal being claimed, the Goal Judge shall decide whether or not the puck/ball has passed between the goal posts, under the crossbar or entirely over the goal line. The decision of the Goal Judge shall be "Goal" or "No Goal," and may be overruled by the Referee.

## Rule 505 Penalty Timekeeper

(a) The "PENALTY TIMEKEEPER" shall keep a correct record of all the penalties assessed by the Referee(s) including the names of the penalized players, the infractions penalized, the duration of each penalty and the time at which each penalty was assessed. The Penalty Timekeeper shall record each penalty shot awarded and the result of the shot.

(b) The Penalty Timekeeper shall check and ensure that the time served by all penalized players is correct. The Penalty Timekeeper shall be responsible for the correct posting of all minor and major penalties on the scoreboard and shall promptly notify the Referee of any discrepancy between the time recorded on the clock and the correct official time.

The Penalty Timekeeper shall, upon request, inform a penalized player of any unexpired penalty time.

Misconduct and coincident minor penalties shall not be recorded on the clock, but such penalized players shall be alerted and released at the first stoppage of play following the expiration of the penalties.

(c) If a player leaves the penalty bench prior to the expiration of the penalty, the Penalty Timekeeper shall note the time and signal the Referee at the next stoppage of play.

## Rule 506 Official Scorer

() The "OFFICIAL SCORER" shall obtain a list of eligible players from each team, prior to the start of the game. This information shall be made known to the Coach of each team. The Official Scorer shall secure the names of the Captain of each team and note such on the Official Score Sheet.

(b)   The Official Scorer shall keep a correct record of all goals scored, and to whom credit shall be given for assists.

  The Official Scorer shall also record the time of entry into the game of any substitute goalkeeper and shall record when a goal has been scored while the goalkeeper has been removed from the playing surface.

(c)   The points for goals and assists shall be announced over the public address system and all changes in such awards shall also be announced.

  No requests for changes in any award of points shall be considered unless they are made at or prior to the conclusion of the game by the team Captain.

(d)   The Official Scorer shall prepare the Official Score Sheet for signature by the Officials and forward it to the League Authorities.

## Rule 507   Game Timekeeper

(a)   The "GAME TIMEKEEPER" shall signal the Referee for the start of each half and the Referee shall start play promptly in accordance with the scheduled playing time. The Game Timekeeper shall record all official playing time.

(b)   If the rink is not equipped with an automatic sound device, or such sound device fails, the Game Timekeeper shall signal the end of play time by blowing a whistle.

(c)   The Game Timekeeper shall announce when one minute of actual playing time remains in each half.

## Rule 508   League Authorities

(a)   The "LEAGUE AUTHORITIES," as applied under these rules, shall be defined as the immediate governing body of the team or teams involved.

# Rules Governing the Game of Inline Hockey

## SECTION SIX

## Playing Rules

## Rule 601  Abuse of Officials and Other Misconduct

(a) Any player who challenges or disputes the ruling of an Official, attempts to incite an opponent or create a disturbance during the game shall be assessed a minor penalty for unsportsmanlike conduct. If the player persists in such conduct, a misconduct penalty shall be assessed and any further persistence by the same player shall result in the assessment of a game misconduct penalty.

In the case of a Coach or other Team Official, a bench minor penalty shall be assessed first and if such conduct continues, a game misconduct penalty shall be assessed.

(b) Any player who shoots the puck/ball after the whistle shall be assessed a minor penalty if, in the opinion of the Referee, the player had sufficient time after the whistle to refrain from taking the shot.

(c) If any player does any of the following, the team shall be assessed a bench minor penalty:

1. In the vicinity of the players' bench, using obscene, profane or abusive language to any person.

2. Throws anything onto the playing surface from the players' bench or penalty bench.

3. Interferes with any Game Official, (non-physically) in the performance of their duties.

(d)  If any player does any of the following, a misconduct penalty shall be assessed:

1. Uses obscene, profane or abusive language to any person before, during or after the game.

2. During a stoppage of play, intentionally shoots or throws the puck/ball out of the reach of an Official who is retrieving it.

3. After being penalized, does not proceed directly to the penalty bench or dressing room when ordered to do so by the Referee. (Equipment shall be delivered to the penalty bench or dressing room by a teammate).

4. Enters and remains in the Referee's Crease, when asked to leave, except for the purpose of skating to the penalty bench.

(e)  If any player does any of the following, a misconduct or game misconduct penalty shall be assessed:

1. Touches or holds any Game Official with the hand or stick.

2. Intentionally bangs the boards, protective glass or goal with a stick at any time.

(f)  If any player does any of the following, a game misconduct penalty shall be assessed:

1. Persists in any course of conduct for which the player has previously been assessed a misconduct penalty.

2. Uses obscene gestures, or racial/ethnic slurs, anywhere in the rink before, during or after the game.

(g) If any player does any of the following, a gross misconduct penalty shall be assessed:

1. Deliberately inflicts or attempts to inflict, physical harm to a Game Official or a Team Official in any manner.

2. Behaves in any manner which is critically detrimental to the conduct of the game including spitting at an opponent, Game Official or Team Official.

(h) If any Team Official does any of the following, the team shall be assessed a bench minor penalty:

1. Bangs the boards with a stick or other instrument at any time.

2. Uses obscene, profane or abusive language to any person before, during or after the game.

3. Throws anything onto the playing surface from the players' bench.

4. Interferes with any Game Official, (non-physically) in the performance of their duties.

5. Attempts to incite an opponent into incurring a penalty.

(i) If any Team Official does any of the following, a game misconduct penalty shall be assessed:

1. Persists in any course of conduct for which the Team Official has previously been assessed a bench minor penalty.

2. Uses obscene gestures, or racial/ethnic slurs, anywhere in the rink before, during or after the game.

(j)  If any Team Official does any of the following, a gross misconduct penalty shall be assessed:

1. Deliberately inflicts or attempts to inflict, physical harm to a Game Official or a Team Official in any manner.

2. Behaves in any manner which is critically detrimental to the conduct of the game including spitting at an opponent, Game Official or Team Official.

## Rule 602  Adjustment to Clothing and Equipment

(a)  Play shall not be stopped or delayed by reason of adjustment of clothing, equipment, skates, or sticks. For a violation of this rule a minor penalty shall be assessed.

(b)  The onus of maintaining clothing and equipment in the proper condition shall be upon the player. If adjustments are required, the player shall retire from the playing surface and play shall continue uninterrupted with a substitute.

(c)  No delay shall be permitted for the repair or adjustment of goalkeeper's equipment. If adjustments are required, the goalkeeper shall retire from the playing surface and be replaced by the substitute or temporary goalkeeper immediately and no warm-up shall be permitted.

For a violation of this rule by a goalkeeper, a minor penalty shall be assessed.

## Rule 603  Attempt to Injure

(a) A match penalty shall be assessed to any player who deliberately attempts to injure an opponent, Official, Coach, or Trainer in any manner, and the circumstances shall be reported to the League Authorities for further action. A substitute for the penalized player shall be permitted at the end of the fifth minute.

## Rule 604  Body-Checking and Boarding

(a) A minor penalty or major plus a game misconduct penalty, at the discretion of the Referee, shall be assessed to any player who intentionally body-checks an opponent, with or without the puck/ball.

(b) A minor penalty or major plus a game misconduct penalty, at the discretion of the Referee, shall be assessed to any player who makes physical contact with an opponent after the whistle has been blown, if, in the opinion of the Referee, the player had sufficient time to avoid such contact.

(c) A minor penalty or major plus a game misconduct penalty, at the discretion of the Referee based upon the degree of violence of the impact with the boards, shall be assessed to any player who fouls an opponent in such a manner that caused the player to be violently thrown into the boards.

"Rolling" an opposing puck/ball carrier along the boards where the player is attempting to go through too small an opening is not boarding.

(d) When a player injures an opponent as the result of "boarding" or "body-checking," the Referee shall assess a major plus a game misconduct penalty to the offending player.

## Rule 605  Broken Stick

(a) A player whose stick is broken may participate in the game provided the broken stick is dropped immediately. A minor penalty shall be assessed for an infraction of this rule.

A broken stick is one which, in the opinion of a Referee, is unfit for normal play.

(b) A goalkeeper may continue to play with a broken stick until the next stoppage of play or until a replacement stick has been legally obtained.

(c) A replacement stick may only be obtained from the players' bench or from a teammate on the playing surface. For a violation of this rule, a bench minor penalty shall be assessed to the team of the offending player, unless a penalty has been assessed under Rule 601 for throwing articles onto the playing surface.

The intent of this rule is to provide for the

assessment of one penalty for one illegal stick replacement.

(d)　A goalkeeper may not go to the players' bench for a replacement stick during a stoppage of play, but must receive a replacement stick from a teammate.

For an infraction of this rule, a minor penalty shall be assessed to the offending goalkeeper.

## Rule 606　Charging and Checking From Behind

(a)　A minor penalty or major plus a game misconduct penalty, at the discretion of the Referee, shall be assessed to a player who runs, jumps into, or charges an opponent.

If more than two steps or strides are taken, it shall be considered "charging."

(b)　A minor penalty or major plus a game misconduct penalty, at the discretion of the Referee, shall be assessed to a player who pushes or body-checks an opponent from behind.

(c)　A minor penalty or a major plus a game misconduct penalty shall be assessed to a player who body-checks or charges a goalkeeper while the goalkeeper is within the goal crease or privileged area.

A goalkeeper is not "fair game" just because the goalkeeper is outside the privileged area. A penalty for interference or charging must be assessed in every case where an opposing player makes unnecessary contact with a goalkeeper.

(d)    When a player injures an opponent as the result of
       "charging" or "checking from behind," the Ref-
       eree shall assess a major plus a game misconduct
       penalty to the offending player.

### Rule 607    Cross-Checking and Butt-Ending

(a)    A minor penalty or major plus a game misconduct
       penalty, at the discretion of the Referee, shall be
       assessed to a player who cross-checks an opponent.

(b)    A minor penalty or major plus a game misconduct
       penalty, at the discretion of the Referee, shall be
       assessed to a player who butt-ends or attempts to
       butt-end an opponent.

       An attempt to butt-end shall include all cases
       in which a butt-end gesture is made, regardless of
       whether body contact is made or not.

(c)    When a player injures an opponent as the result of
       "cross-checking" or "butt-ending," the Referee
       shall assess a major plus a game misconduct
       penalty to the offending player.

(d)    Butt-ending may also be treated as a match
       penalty under attempt to injure or deliberate
       injury to an opponent.

### Rule 608    Deliberate Injury to Opponents
             and Head-Butting

(a)    A match penalty shall be assessed to a player who
       deliberately injures an opponent, Team Official or
       Game Official in any manner, and the circum-

stances shall be reported to the League Authorities for further action.

(b) No substitute shall be permitted to take the place of the penalized player until after five minutes actual playing time have elapsed, from the time the penalty was assessed.

(c) A match penalty shall be assessed to a player who deliberately head-butts an opponent, Team Official or Game Official, and the circumstances shall be reported to the League Authorities for further action.

### Rule 609   Delaying the Game

(a) A minor penalty shall be assessed to any player or goalkeeper, who delays the game by deliberately shooting, batting or throwing the puck/ball outside the playing area.

This penalty shall also be assessed when it occurs during a stoppage of play.

Intentional delay of the game by a goalkeeper shall be assessed at the discretion of the Referee.

(b) A minor penalty shall be assessed to a player or goalkeeper who delays the game by deliberately displacing the goal post from its normal position. Play shall be stopped immediately when the goal post has been displaced.

If a goalkeeper deliberately displaces the goal post or deliberately removes the helmet or face mask during the course of a breakaway by the attacking team, a penalty shot shall be awarded to the non-offending team. The penalty shot shall be taken by the player last in possession of the puck/ball.

(c) A bench minor penalty shall be assessed to any team which, after a warning by the Referee, fails to place the correct number of players on the playing surface, thereby causing a delay in any manner.

(d) A minor penalty shall be assessed to a player who, after a warning by the Referee, fails to maintain a proper position during the face-off.

## Rule 610 Elbowing and Kneeing

(a) A minor penalty or major plus a game misconduct penalty shall be assessed to any player who uses the elbow or knee in such a manner as to foul an opponent, in any way.

(b) When a player injures an opponent as the result of "elbowing" or "kneeing," the Referee shall assess a major plus a game misconduct penalty to the offending player.

## Rule 611 Face-Offs

(a) The puck/ball shall be "faced-off" by the Referee or the Linesman dropping the puck/ball onto the playing surface between the sticks of the two players facing-off. Players facing off shall stand facing their opponent's end of the rink with the blade of their sticks in contact with the nearest white area of the face-off spot and clear of the red center area of the spot. The attacking team player shall be the first player to place the stick on the playing surface.

If a player facing-off fails to take the proper position immediately when directed by the Official, the Official may order a replacement for that face-off by a teammate on the playing surface.

No other player shall be allowed to enter the face-off circle or come within 15 feet of the players facing-off the puck/ball, and they must stand on-side on all face-offs.

When a player, other than the player facing-off, fails to maintain the proper position, the center of the offending team shall be ejected from the face-off.

For a second violation of any of the provisions of this rule, a minor penalty shall be assessed to the player who commits the second violation.

No substitution of players shall be permitted until the face-off has been completed and play has been resumed except when any penalty is assessed during the face-off.

The whistle shall not be blown to start play. Playing time shall commence from the instant the puck/ball is faced-off and shall stop when the whistle is blown.

b) If, after a warning by the Official, either of the players fails to take the proper position for the face-off promptly, the Official shall be entitled to conduct the face-off regardless of such default.

c) During the conduct of any face-off, no player shall make any physical contact with an opponent except in the course of playing the puck/ball after the face-off has been completed.

For a violation of this rule the Referee shall assess a minor penalty to the player whose action caused the physical contact.

"Conduct of any face-off" commences when the Official designates the spot of the face-off and takes up a position to drop the puck/ball.

(d) No face-off shall be conducted at a location other than at a face-off spot.

(e) When a stoppage of play occurs between the end zone face-off spots and the near end of the rink, the ensuing face-off shall take place at the end face-off spot on the side where the stoppage occurred, unless otherwise provided in these rules.

(f) When a violation of a rule has been committed, or a stoppage of play has been caused by any player of the attacking team in the Attacking Zone, the ensuing face-off shall take place at the nearest high zone face-off spot.

This includes a stoppage of play caused by a player of the attacking team shooting the puck/ball onto the back of the defending team's goal without any intervening action by the defending team.

(g) When a violation of a rule has been committed or a stoppage of play has been caused by players of both teams, the ensuing face-off shall take place at the nearest face-off spot (excluding center face-off spot) to where the puck/ball was when the stoppage occurred.

(h)   When a goal is legally scored, the ensuing face-off shall be conducted at the center face-off spot.

(i)   When the game is stopped for any reason not specifically covered in the Official Playing Rules, the ensuing face-off shall take place at the nearest face-off spot to where the puck/ball was last played.

## Rule 612   Falling on Puck/Ball

(a)   A minor penalty shall be assessed to a player, other than a goalkeeper, who deliberately falls on or gathers the puck/ball into the body or who holds the puck/ball against any part of the goal or the boards.

Any player who drops to block a shot shall not be penalized if the puck/ball is shot under the player or becomes lodged in any clothing or equipment. A minor penalty shall be assessed to any player who uses the hands to obtain such stoppage.

(b)   A minor penalty shall be assessed to a goalkeeper who falls on or gathers the puck/ball into the body, when the body is entirely outside the boundaries of the privileged area or who falls on or gathers the puck/ball into the body, when the body is entirely outside the goal crease and the puck/ball is behind the goal line.

A minor penalty shall be assessed to a goalkeeper who holds the puck/ball against any part of the goal or the boards.

(c) No defending player, except the goalkeeper, shall be permitted to fall on the puck/ball, hold the puck/ball, or gather a puck/ball into the body or hands when the puck/ball is within the goal crease.

For a violation of this rule, play shall be immediately stopped and a penalty shot shall be awarded to the non-offending team. However, if the goalkeeper has been removed from the playing surface when the infraction occurs, a goal shall be awarded to the non-offending team in lieu of the penalty shot.

This rule shall be interpreted so that a penalty shot shall be awarded only when the puck/ball is in the goal crease at the instant the infraction occurs. However, in cases where the puck/ball is outside the goal crease, Rule 612 (a) may still be applied and a minor penalty assessed, even though no penalty shot is awarded.

### Rule 613   Fighting

(a) A major penalty shall be assessed to any player who is involved in a fight on or off the playing surface before, during or after the game.

(b) A minor or a double minor penalty shall be assessed to a player who, having been struck, retaliates with a punch or an attempted punch. However, at the discretion of the Referee, a major penalty shall be assessed if the player continues the altercation.

The Referee is provided with very wide latitude in regard to the penalties which may be assessed under this rule. This is done to enable the Referee to differentiate between the obvious degrees of responsibility of the participants either for, starting the fight, or persisting in continuing the fight.

Referees are directed to employ every means provided by these rules to prevent "brawling."

(c) Any player receiving a major penalty for fisticuffs shall automatically be assessed a game misconduct penalty.

(d) A game misconduct penalty shall be assessed to any player or goalkeeper who is the first to intervene in a fighting altercation already in progress. This penalty is in addition to any other penalty incurred in the same incident.

(e) A game misconduct penalty shall be assessed to any player who resists the Game Officials in the discharge of their duties during an altercation.

(f) A minor penalty shall be assessed to a goalkeeper who leaves the immediate vicinity of the goal crease to participate in an altercation. This penalty shall be in addition to any penalty incurred during the altercation.

## Rule 614 Goals and Assists

*(Note) It is the responsibility of the Referee to award goals and assists, and such decision is final.*

*In cases of an obvious error in awarding a goal or an assist which has been announced, it should*

*be corrected promptly. Changes shall not be made
on the scoring summary after the Referee has
signed the Official Score Sheet.*

(a) A goal shall be scored when the puck/ball has
been put between the goal posts by the stick of a
player of the attacking team from in front, below
the cross bar and entirely across the goal line,
before playing time expires.

A "goal" shall be credited in the scoring records
to a player who shall have propelled the puck/ball
into the opponent's goal. Each "goal" shall count
as one point in the player's record.

An "assist" shall be credited to the player or
players taking part in the play immediately pre-
ceding the goal, but no more than two assists can
be credited on any goal.

Only one point can be credited to any one
player for any one goal scored.

(b) A goal shall be scored if the puck/ball is put into
the goal in any way by a player of the defending
team. The player of the attacking team who last
played the puck/ball shall be credited with the
goal, but no assist shall be awarded.

(c) If an attacking player kicks the puck/ball and the
puck/ball goes directly into the goal or is deflected
into the goal by any player, including the goalkeeper, the goal shall not be allowed.

(d) If the puck/ball is deflected into the goal from the
shot of an attacking player by striking any part of
any player, the goal shall be allowed. The player

who deflected the puck/ball shall be credited with the goal. The goal shall not be allowed if the puck/ball has been kicked, thrown, or otherwise deliberately directed by an attacking player into the goal by any means other than a stick.

(e) If a goal is scored as a result of a puck/ball being deflected directly into the goal off an Official, the goal shall not be allowed.

(f) Should a player legally propel the puck/ball into the goal crease of the opposing team and the puck/ball becomes loose in the goal crease and available to a player of the attacking team, any goal scored on the play shall be allowed.

(g) Any goal scored, other than as covered by the Official Playing Rules, shall not be allowed.

## Rule 615 Gross Misconduct

(a) A Referee may suspend from the game any player, Manager, Coach, or Trainer guilty of gross misconduct of any kind and must report the incident to the League Authorities.

## Rule 616 Handling Puck/Ball with Hands

(a) If a player, other than a goalkeeper, closes the hand on the puck/ball, play shall be stopped and a face-off shall follow; however, if the puck/ball is dropped immediately, play shall be allowed to continue.

If a goalkeeper holds the puck/ball with the hand for more than three seconds, play shall be stopped and a face-off shall follow; however, after an initial warning by the Referee, a goalkeeper who holds the puck/ball unnecessarily shall be assessed a minor penalty for delaying the game.

(b)   A goalkeeper shall not intentionally drop the puck/ball into the pads or onto the goal net nor deliberately pile obstacles at the goal that, in the opinion of the Referee, would tend to prevent the scoring of a goal.

   The object of this rule is to keep the puck/ball in play continuously and any action taken by the goalkeeper which causes an unnecessary stoppage shall be penalized.

   For a violation of this rule, a minor penalty shall be assessed to the offending player.

(c)   If a goalkeeper throws the puck/ball forward toward the opponent's goal and it is first played by a teammate, play shall be stopped and the ensuing face-off shall be conducted at the nearest end zone face-off spot of the offending team.

(d)   If a defending player, other than the goalkeeper, picks up the puck/ball in the goal crease from the playing surface with the hands, or holds the puck/ball while it is in the goal crease, the play shall be stopped immediately and a penalty shot shall be awarded to the non-offending team.

   If the above situation occurs while the goalkeeper is off the playing surface, a goal shall be awarded to the non-offending team.

(e)     A player shall be permitted to stop or "bat" the
        puck/ball in the air with the hand, or push it along
        the playing surface with the hand, and play shall
        not be stopped unless the puck/ball has been
        deliberately directed to a teammate in the Attack-
        ing Zone, in which case the play shall be stopped
        and the puck/ball faced off at the nearest high
        zone face-off spot.

(f)     A goal that is scored as the result of the puck/ball
        being propelled by the hand of an attacking player
        and entered the goal either directly or after deflect-
        ing off any player including the goalkeeper, shall
        not be allowed.

## Rule 617  High Sticks

(a)     The carrying of the stick above the normal height
        of the shoulders is prohibited. The Referee shall
        assess a minor penalty or a major plus a game mis-
        conduct penalty to any player who strikes an
        opponent with a stick so carried.
            The use of the "slap shot" in the 10-and-Under
        age division and below is prohibited. A face-off
        shall take place at an end zone face-off spot of the
        offending player's team who, in the process of
        making a shot or pass, raises the blade of the stick
        above the waist in the back swing of such shot.

(b)     When a player injures an opponent as the result of
        "high sticking," the Referee shall assess a major
        plus a game misconduct penalty to the offending
        player.

(c) A goal scored by an attacking player who strikes the puck/ball with the stick which is carried above the height of the goal frame cross bar, shall not be allowed.

(d) Batting the puck/ball above the normal height of the shoulders with the stick is prohibited and when it occurs play shall be stopped and the ensuing face-off shall take place at an end zone face-off spot of the offending player's team unless:

1. The puck/ball is batted to an opponent, in which case the play shall continue.

2. A player of the defending team shall bat the puck/ball into the player's own goal, in which case the goal shall be allowed.

## Rule 618  Holding an Opponent

(a) A minor penalty shall be assessed to a player who holds an opponent with the hands, legs, feet, stick, or in any other way.

(b) A minor or major penalty shall be assessed to any player who grabs or holds the face mask of an opponent with the hand.

(c) When a player injures an opponent as the result of "holding the face mask," the Referee shall assess a major plus a game misconduct penalty to the offending player.

## Rule 619  Hooking

(a)  A minor penalty shall be assessed to a player who impedes or seeks to impede the progress of an opponent by hooking with the stick.

(b)  When a player injures an opponent as the result of "hooking," the Referee shall assess a major plus a game misconduct penalty to the offending player.

## Rule 620  Illegal Clearing (Icing)

No such rule.

## Rule 621  Interference

(a)  A minor penalty shall be assessed to any player who interferes with or impedes the progress of an opponent who is not in possession of the puck/ball, deliberately knocks a stick out of an opponent's hand, prevents a player who has dropped the stick or any other piece of equipment from regaining possession of it, or shoots a stick or other object toward an opponent.

The last player to touch the puck/ball shall be considered to be the player in possession.

(b)  A minor penalty shall be assessed to any player on the players' or the penalty bench who, by means of the stick or body, interferes with the movements of the puck/ball or an opponent on the playing surface during the progress of play.

(c)  A minor penalty shall be assessed to any player who, by means of the stick or body, interferes

(d) Unless the puck/ball is in the goal crease area, a player of the attacking team may not stand on the goal crease line or in the goal crease or hold the stick in the goal crease. If the puck/ball should enter the goal while such a condition prevails, a goal shall not be allowed. For a violation of this rule, while the attacking team has possession of the puck/ball, play shall be stopped and the ensuing face-off shall take place at the nearest high zone face-off spot.

This rule shall not apply when the goalkeeper is out of the goal crease.

(e) If a player of the attacking team has been pushed or otherwise physically forced into the goal crease by an opposing player, and the puck/ball should enter the goal while the player so interfered with is still in the goal crease, the goal shall be allowed.

(f) When the goalkeeper has been removed from the playing surface and any member of the same team not legally on the playing surface interferes by means of the body, stick, or any other object with the movements of the puck/ball or an opposing player, the Referee shall immediately award a goal to the non-offending team.

*(Note) The attention of Referees is directed partic ularly to three types of offensive interference which shall be penalized.*

1. When the defending team secures possession of the puck/ball in its own zone and the other members of the same team run interference for the puck/ball carrier by forming a protective screen against forecheckers.

2. When a player facing-off obstructs an opponent after the face-off when the opponent is not in possession of the puck/ball.

3. When the puck/ball carrier makes a drop pass and follows through so as to make body contact with an opposing player.

## Rule 622 Interference by Spectators

(a) In the event of a player being held or interfered with by a spectator, the Referee shall immediately stop the play, unless the team of the player being interfered with is in possession of the puck/ball at the time, in which case the play shall be allowed to be completed. The ensuing face-off shall take place at the nearest face-off spot to where the puck/ball was last played.

(b) Any player who physically interferes with a spectator shall be assessed a game misconduct penalty and the circumstances shall be reported to the League Authorities for further action.

(c) In the event that objects are thrown onto the playing surface which interfere with the progress of the game, the Referee shall stop the play and the ensuing face-off shall take place at the nearest face-off spot to where the puck/ball was last played.

## Rule 623 Kicking Player

(a) A match penalty shall be assessed to a player who kicks or attempts to kick another player. A substitute shall be permitted at the end of the fifth minute.

## Rule 624 Kicking Puck/Ball

(a) Kicking the puck/ball shall be permitted in all zones; however, a goal that is scored as the result of the puck/ball being kicked by an attacking player and entered the goal either directly or after deflecting off any player including the goalkeeper, shall not be allowed.

## Rule 625 Leaving Player or Penalty Benches

(a) No player may leave the players' bench or penalty bench at any time during an altercation. Substitutions made prior to the start of the altercation shall not be penalized under this rule provided the players so substituting do not enter the altercation.

A double minor penalty plus a game misconduct penalty shall be assessed to the player who was the first to leave the players' or penalty bench during an altercation. If players of both teams leave their respective benches at the same time, the first identifiable player of each team shall be penalized under this rule.

For the purposes of determining which player was the first to leave the players' bench during an altercation, the Referee may consult with the Linesmen or other Game Officials.

Any player who leaves the players' bench during an altercation and is assessed a minor, major or misconduct penalty for such actions, shall also be assessed a game misconduct penalty.

Other players who leave the players' bench or penalty bench during an altercation shall be assessed a misconduct penalty (maximum 5 per team).

If a player illegally enters the game, any goal scored by that team while the illegal player is on the playing surface shall be disallowed, but all penalties assessed to either team shall be served as regular penalties.

(b) Except at the end of each period, or upon the expiration of a penalty, no player may leave the penalty bench, at any time.

A penalized player who leaves the penalty bench prior to the expiration of the penalty, whether play is in progress or not, shall be assessed an additional minor penalty after serving the unexpired penalty time.

When a player leaves the penalty bench prior to the expiration of the penalty, the Penalty Timekeeper shall note the time and verbally alert the Referee who shall stop play when the offending player's team gains possession and control of the puck.

In the case of a player returning to the playing surface prior to the expiration of the penalty, through an error of the Penalty Timekeeper, the player is not to serve an additional penalty, but must serve the unexpired time.

A penalized player who leaves the penalty bench during an altercation shall be assessed a minor penalty plus a game misconduct penalty, in addition to any unexpired time.

When a penalized player returns to the playing surface from the penalty bench prior to the expiration of the penalty, any goal scored by that team, while the player is illegally on the playing surface, shall be disallowed, but all penalties assessed to either team shall be served as regular penalties.

(c) If a player of the attacking team in possession of the puck/ball shall be in a position as to have no opposing player to pass other than the goalkeeper, and is interfered with by a player who has entered the game illegally, the attacking player shall be awarded a penalty shot.

If the opposing goalkeeper is off the playing surface and the attacking player is interfered with by an illegal player, a goal shall be awarded to the non-offending team.

(d) If a Team Official steps onto the playing surface after the start of a half and before that half is completed without the permission of the Referee, the Referee shall assess a bench minor penalty to the team of the offending Coach.

(e)     During any face-off, if a team starts with fewer
        players than entitled to, any player subsequently
        entering the game shall not be eligible to play any
        puck/ball coming from the Defending Zone while
        the player is in the Attacking Zone unless the
        puck/ball is first played by another player in the
        Attacking Zone.

### Rule 626  Off-Sides

No such rule.

### Rule 627  Passes

(a)     The puck/ball may be passed by any player to any
        player of the same team within any of the two
        zones into which the rink is divided and may be
        passed forward by a player in the Defending Zone
        to a teammate over the center red line.

### Rule 628  Puck/Ball Must be Kept in Motion

(a)     The puck/ball must be kept in motion at all times.
        Play shall not be stopped because the puck/ball is
        frozen along the boards by two or more opposing
        players, unless one of the players falls onto the
        puck/ball. If one player freezes the puck/ball along
        the boards or if a player deliberately falls on the
        puck/ball a minor penalty shall be assessed for
        delaying the game.  However, the Referee may
        stop the play along the boards if allowing play to
        continue shall lead to unnecessary contact sur-
        rounding the puck/ball.

## Rule 629 Puck/Ball or Player Out of Bounds or Unplayable

(a)   When the puck/ball goes outside the playing area or strikes any obstacles above the playing surface other than the boards, glass or wire, it shall be faced-off at the nearest face-off spot to where it was last played.

When the puck/ball becomes unplayable due to a defect in the rink, it shall be faced-off at the nearest face-off spot to where it was last played. However, if the puck/ball is shot out of the rink by the attacking team, the face-off shall be at the nearest high zone face-off spot.

(b)   When the puck/ball becomes lodged in the netting on the outside of the goal or if it is frozen between opposing players, the Referee shall stop play and face-off the puck/ball at the nearest face-off spot to where it was last played unless, in the opinion of the Referee the stoppage was caused by a player of the attacking team, in which case the ensuing face-off shall be conducted at the nearest high zone face-off spot.

The defending team and/or the attacking team may play the puck/ball off the net at any time. However, should the puck/ball remain on the net for longer than three seconds, play shall be stopped and the face-off shall take place at the nearest end zone face-off spot, except when the stoppage is caused by a player of the attacking team, in which case the ensuing face-off shall be conducted at the nearest high zone face-off spot.

If the puck/ball comes to rest on top of the goal frame, the play shall be stopped immediately.

(c) A minor penalty shall be assessed to a goalkeeper who deliberately drops the puck/ball on the goal netting to cause a stoppage of play.

(d) If the puck/ball comes to rest on top of the boards surrounding the playing area, it shall be considered to be in play and may be played legally by the hand or stick.

(e) In temporary rinks, all players on the playing surface must remain within the confines of the playing surface while the puck/ball is in play. The play shall be stopped immediately whenever a player jumps over the boundary and out of bounds.

If, in the opinion of the Referee, a player intentionally jumps out of bounds for the purpose of obtaining a stoppage of play, a minor penalty for delaying the game shall be assessed.

## Rule 630 Puck/Ball Out of Sight and Illegal Puck/Ball

(a) Should a scramble take place, or a player accidentally falls on the puck/ball and it is out of the sight of the Referee, play shall be stopped immediately. The ensuing face-off shall take place at the nearest face-off spot, unless otherwise provided for in the rules.

(b) If, at any time during play, a puck/ball other than the one officially in play shall appear on the playing surface, which interferes with the progress of the game, the play shall be stopped immediately.

## Rule 631  Puck/Ball Striking Official

(a) Play shall not be stopped because the puck/ball touches an Official anywhere on the rink.

## Rule 632  Refusing to Start Play

(a) If, when both teams are on the playing surface, one team for any reason shall refuse to play when ordered to do so by the Referee, the Captain shall be warned and the team so refusing shall be allowed 15 seconds to begin the game or resume play. If, at the end of that time the team shall still refuse to play, the Referee shall assess a bench minor penalty to the offending team.

Should there be a reoccurrence of the same incident, the Referee shall suspend the game, and the circumstances shall be reported to the League Authorities for further action.

(b) If a team, when ordered to do so by the Referee, fails to go onto the playing surface promptly, it shall be assessed a bench minor penalty.

If the team shall still refuse to go onto the playing surface and start play within five minutes, the Referee shall suspend the game, and the circumstances shall be reported to the League Authorities for further action.

## Rule 633 Slashing

(a)    A minor penalty or major plus a game misconduct penalty, at the discretion of the Referee, shall be assessed to any player who slashes or attempts to slash an opponent with the stick.

    Referees should penalize as "slashing" any player who swings the stick at an opponent (whether in or out of range) without actually making contact, or when a player on the pretext of playing the puck/ball makes a wild swing at the puck/ball with the intent to intimidate an opponent.

(b)    When a player injures an opponent as the result of "slashing," the Referee shall assess a major plus a game misconduct penalty to the offending player.

(c)    Any player who swings the stick at another player during the course of any altercation shall be subject to a match penalty, and the circumstances shall be reported to the League Authorities for further action.

(d)    A minor penalty shall be assessed to any player who makes stick contact with the opposing goalkeeper, in the goal crease, who has covered or caught the puck/ball, regardless of whether or not the Referee has stopped the play.

## Rule 634 Spearing

(a)    A minor penalty or major plus a game misconduct penalty, at the discretion of the Referee, shall be assessed to a player who spears or attempts to spear an opponent.

Attempt to spear shall include all cases where a spearing gesture is made regardless of whether body contact is made or not.

(b)     When a player injures an opponent as the result of "spearing," the Referee shall assess a major plus a game misconduct penalty to the offending player.

(c)     Spearing may also be treated as a match penalty under attempt to injure or deliberate injury to an opponent.

## Rule 635   Start of Game and Periods

(a)     The game shall start at the time scheduled by a face-off at the center face-off spot and shall be promptly resumed for the second half in the same manner.

(b)     Each team shall defend the goal furthest from its players' bench to start the game. The teams shall change ends after the first half only.

(c)     During the pre-game warm-up and before each half, each team shall confine its activity to its own end of the rink. All players must wear full equipment during warm-ups and during the handshake following the game.

(d)     It is recommended that when both teams are to leave the playing surface through a common exit, the team whose players' bench closest to the exit leave first. The home team should enter the playing surface first.

(e)    When a team fails to appear on the playing surface
       without a proper justification, an Official shall
       warn the team that it must enter the playing sur-
       face immediately. If the team fails to do so
       promptly, the Referee shall assess a bench minor
       penalty for Delaying the Game.

## Rule 636 Throwing Stick

(a)    When any player or Team Official of the defending
       team deliberately throws or shoots a stick or any
       other object at the puck/ball in the Defending
       Zone, the Referee shall allow the play to be com-
       pleted and if a goal is not scored, a penalty shot
       shall be awarded to the fouled player.

       If, however, the goal is unattended and the
       attacking player has no defending player to pass
       and has a chance to score on an open goal, and a
       stick or any other object is thrown or shot at the
       puck/ball by a member of the defending team,
       thereby preventing a shot on the open goal, a goal
       shall be awarded to the non-offending team.

b)     A minor penalty shall be assessed to any player on
       the playing surface who throws or shoots a stick
       or any other object in the direction of the
       puck/ball in any zone except when such act has
       been penalized by a penalty shot or awarded goal.

       When a player discards a broken stick by toss-
       ing it to the side of the rink (and not over the
       boards) in such a way that shall not interfere with
       play or an opposing player, no penalty shall be
       assessed for doing so.

(c)   A misconduct penalty shall be assessed to any
player who throws a stick or any part thereof outside the playing area. A game misconduct penalty
shall be assessed to any player who deliberately
throws a stick or any part thereof outside the playing area at or in the direction of any spectators.

## Rule 637   Time of Match and Time-Outs

(a)   A game shall consist of two 15-25 minute halves.
Leagues have the jurisdiction to set the length of
each half (running time or stop time) based on the
amount of time designated to complete the game.
For all State, Regional and National Championship games, 15 minute stop time halves shall be
played.

   If running time is used and the score is within
one goal, or tied, stop time shall be played during
the last two minutes of play.

   A two-minute rest period shall be permitted
between halves, after which the teams shall
change ends.

(b)   The team scoring the greater number of goals during the two halves shall be declared the winner, and
shall be credited with two points in the standings.

(c)   The Referee may order the game to be suspended
anytime the playing area is deemed to be in an
unsafe condition. The game shall remain suspended until such condition is corrected. Referees
are particularly cautioned about wet playing surfaces and should take the overly-cautious

approach when determining whether or not play-ing conditions are safe.

*(Note) Leagues shall have the authority to deter-mine their own policies regarding weather related delays or cancellations.*

If any unusual delay occurs during the first half, the Referee may order the intermission to take place immediately and the balance of the half shall be completed upon the resumption of play with the teams defending the same goals, after which the teams shall change ends and resume play of the second half without delay.

(d) Each team shall be permitted to take one time-out of a one minute duration which must be taken during a stoppage of play. If running time is played, the clock shall be stopped during a time out. The clock shall be restarted upon the con-ducting of the ensuing face-off.

During a time-out, all players on the playing surface may proceed to their respective players' bench. Any penalized player must remain in the penalty bench during a time-out.

A time-out may not be used to warm-up a goal-keeper.

## Rule 638 Tied Games

a) If, at the end of two halves, the score is tied, the game shall be declared a tie. No overtime period shall be played unless it is necessary to determine a winner.

(b)    In Tournament and Play-Off games in which it is
       necessary to determine a winner for advancement,
       the following shall take place:

       1. A two minute rest period shall follow.

       2. The teams shall not change ends.

       3. A five minute overtime period shall be played.

       4. The game shall terminate upon the scoring of a
          goal and the team scoring the goal shall be
          declared the winner.

       If no team scores during the overtime period, a
       shoot-out shall take place as follows:
          Four players from each team shall be selected to
       participate in a series of penalty shot attempts.
       The players shall alternate attempts, with the vis-
       iting team having the first attempt. Any player or
       team Official whose penalty has not expired at the
       end of overtime play shall not be allowed to par-
       ticipate in the shoot out and must leave the arena
       immediately following the overtime period.
          Teams may change goalkeepers only at the
       beginning of the shoot-out or if a goalkeeper is
       injured during the shoot-out. Goalkeepers shall
       not change goals during the shoot-out.
          After all eight players have taken their shot, the
       team scoring the most goals shall be declared the
       winner.
          Should neither team have an advantage at the
       end of the first shoot-out round, a second shoot-out
       round shall take place, in which case, the four

players from each team from the first shoot-out round shall be eligible to participate. The second shoot-out round shall be a sudden-victory format in which each team has one penalty shot attempt to score. All non-penalized, non-injured players, excluding goalkeepers, on a team shall shoot before that team shall be allowed to have a player shoot for a second time during the same shoot-out round.

If, after one player from each team has shot, only one team has scored, that team shall be declared the winner. If, after one player from each team has shot and the score remains tied, the procedure shall be repeated until one team scores while its opponents do not.

Goals scored during the shoot-out rounds shall not count toward a player's scoring statistics. Goals scored against a goalkeeper shall not count toward the goalkeeper's statistics. Goalkeepers shall receive either a win or a loss based on the results of the shoot-out.

All rules applicable during the taking of a penalty shot shall also apply during the shoot-out.

(c)   Any overtime period shall be considered to be a part of the game and all unexpired penalties shall remain in force.

### Rule 639   Tripping

(a)   A minor penalty shall be assessed to any player who places the stick, leg, knee, foot, arm, hand, or elbow in such a manner that it causes an opponent to trip or fall.

If, in the opinion of the Referee, a player is unquestionably hook-checking the puck/ball and obtains possession of it, thereby tripping the opposing player, no penalty shall be assessed.

Accidental trips that occur simultaneously with the whistle shall not be penalized.

Any player who deliberately dives onto the playing surface, except to block a shot, contacts an opponent and causes the player to trip or fall, shall be assessed a minor penalty.

(b) When a player, in possession and control of the puck/ball in the Attacking Zone and having no opponent to pass other than the goalkeeper, is tripped or otherwise fouled from behind, thus preventing a reasonable scoring opportunity, a penalty shot shall be awarded to the non-offending team. The Referee shall not stop the play until the attacking team has lost possession and control of the puck/ball to the defending team.

The intent of this rule is to restore a reasonable scoring opportunity which has been lost by reason of a foul from behind when the foul is committed on the opponent's side of the center red line.

"Possession and control" of the puck/ball means the act of propelling the puck/ball with a stick. If, while it is being propelled, the puck/ball is touched by another player, hits the goal or goes free, the player shall no longer be considered to be "in possession and control" of the puck/ball.

(c) If, when the opposing goalkeeper has been removed from the playing surface, a player in possession and control of the puck/ball is tripped or otherwise fouled with no opposing player to pass, thus preventing a reasonable scoring opportunity, the Referee shall immediately stop play and award a goal to the non-offending team.

## Rule 640 Unnecessary Roughness (Roughing)

(a) At the discretion of the Referee, a minor or double minor penalty may be assessed to any player who uses unnecessary roughness against an opponent.

(b) A minor penalty for unnecessary roughness must be assessed every time an opposing player makes unnecessary physical contact with the player in possession of the puck/ball.

It is not the intent to penalize incidental contact between two opposing players who are actively in pursuit of the puck/ball. The act of riding an opponent off the puck/ball shall not be considered to be roughing. However, this does not allow the player without the puck/ball to throw their body into the opponent to achieve possession.

# Rules Governing the Game of Inline Hockey

## Summary
## of
## Penalties

The following summary of penalties is intended for general application of the rules. Specific situations may require different applications. All referenced rules should be consulted for exact language.

## Personal Fouls (Minor Penalty)

| | |
|---|---|
| 202 (d) | Leaving players' bench to protest call |
| 301 (e) | Participating with more then one stick |
| 601 (a) | Unsportsmanlike conduct |
| 601 (b) | Shooting puck/ball after whistle |
| 611 (c) | Face-off interference |
| 618 (a) | Holding |
| 619 (a) | Hooking |
| 621 (a) | Interference |
| 621 (b) | Interference by player on bench |
| 621 (c) | Interfering with goalkeeper in crease |
| 625 (b) | Leaving penalty bench prematurely |
| 633 (d) | Stick contact with goalkeeper |
| 639 (a) | Tripping |

## Delay of Game, Player or Goalkeeper

| | |
|---|---|
| 602 (a, c) | Adjusting clothing/equipment |
| 609 (a) | Deliberately shooting/batting puck/ball out of rink |
| 609 (b) | Deliberate goal displacement (non-breakaway) |
| 609 (d) | Continued improper face-off position |
| 611 (a) | Second face-off violation, same team |
| 612 (a) | Deliberately falling on puck/ball (outside of goal crease) |
| 628 (a) | Freezing puck/ball along boards |
| 629 (e) | Intentionally jumping out of bounds in temporary rinks |

## Goalkeeper Infractions

| | |
|---|---|
| 303 (b, c) | Wearing illegal equipment |
| 304 (c) | Deliberately removing helmet/facemask (non-breakaway) |
| 407 (e) | Participating in play across center red line |
| 605 (d) | Going to bench for stick at stoppage |
| 612 (b) | Deliberately falling on puck/ball outside of privileged area |
| 613 (f) | Leaving goal crease during altercation |
| 616 (a) | Holding puck/ball more then 3 seconds |
| 616 (b) | Piling up obstacles in front of goal |
| 629 (c) | Dropping puck/ball into goal netting |

## Stick and Equipment Violations

| | |
|---|---|
| 301 (d) | Playing with an illegal stick |
| 304 (c) | Playing without helmet/facemask |
| 305 (b) | Playing with cut palm on glove |
| 605 (a) | Playing with broken stick |
| 636 (b) | Throwing a stick (non-Penalty Shot) |

## Bench Minor

| | |
|---|---|
| 205 (a) | Too many players on the playing surface |
| 205 (c) | Illegal entry from penalty bench |
| 205 (d) | Goalkeeper to bench at stoppage |
| 308 (b) | Stick or equipment measurement legal |
| 308 (e) | Measurement request for delaying the game purpose |
| 601 (c1, h2) | Obscene, profane, or abusive language from bench |
| 601 (c2, h3) | Articles thrown onto the playing surface from players' bench |

601 (c3, h4)
  Non-physical interference with Game Official
601 (h1)   Bangs boards with stick (Team Official)
601 (h5)   Attempts to incite opponent (Team Official)
605 (c)    Receiving illegal stick
609 (c)    Continued incorrect players on playing surface
625 (d)    Team Official on surface without permission
632 (a)    Refusing to start play
632 (b)    Refusing to go onto playing surface

## Minor or Double Minor

640 (a, b)  Unnecessary roughness

## Minor or Major plus Game Misconduct

604 (a)    Body-checking
604 (b)    Avoidable physical contact after whistle
604 (c)    Boarding
606 (a)    Charging
606 (b)    Checking from behind
606 (c)    Body-checking goalkeeper within privileged area
607 (a)    Cross-checking
610 (a)    Elbowing/kneeing
617 (a)    High-sticking
618 (b)    Holding or grabbing facemask
633 (a)    Slashing

## Minor plus Misconduct

308 (c)    Refusing to surrender equipment for measurement

## Minor plus Game Misconduct

625 (b)    Leaving penalty bench during altercation

---

## Minor, Double Minor, or Major plus Game Misconduct
613 (b, c)  Fisticuffs (Retaliation)

## Double Minor plus Game Misconduct
625 (a)  First to leave bench during a fighting altercation

## Minor, Major plus Game Misconduct, or Match Penalty
607 (b, d)  Butt-ending
634 (a, c)  Spearing

## Major plus Game Misconduct
613 (a, c)  Fisticuffs
619 (b)  Hooking with injury

## Misconduct Penalty
304 (a)  2nd equipment violation (including mouth guard)
304 (d)  Helmet/facemask not worn on bench
601 (a)  Persisting in unsportsmanlike conduct
601 (d1)  Obscene, profane, abusive language (player)
601 (d2)  Puck/ball shot away from Game Official retrieving it
601 (d3)  Not proceeding to penalty bench or dressing room
601 (d4)  Player in referee crease

## Misconduct or Game Misconduct
601 (e1)  Touches/holds Game Official with stick or hand
601 (e2)  Bangs boards or glass with stick (player)
636 (c)  Stick thrown out of playing area

## Misconduct plus Game Misconduct
625 (a)  Leaving bench during altercation (max. 5 per team)

## Game Misconduct

601 (a, f1, i1)
   Persisting in unsportsmanlike conduct
601 (f2, i2)
   Obscene gestures (players or Team Officials)
613 (d)   First to intervene in fighting altercation
613 (e)   Resisting Game Officials in the discharge of their duties
622 (b)   Player interference with spectator

## Match Penalty

603 (a)   Attempt to injure opponent
608 (a)   Deliberate injury of opponent
608 (c)   Head-butting
623 (a)   Kicking opponent
633 (c)   Swinging stick at opponent in altercation

## Gross Misconduct

601 (g1, j1)
   Injury or attempting to injure Game Official or Team Official
601 (g2, j2)
   Detrimental behavior (player or Team Official)

## Penalty Shot

609 (b)   Goalkeeper deliberately displaces goal (breakaway)
609 (b)   Deliberate removal of goalkeeper's helmet/facemask (breakaway)

## Penalty Shot or Awarded Goal

612 (c)   Player falling on puck/ball in crease
616 (d)   Player picking up puck/ball from crease

| 625 (c) | Illegal entry (breakaway) |
| 636 (a) | Stick thrown at puck/ball in defending zone |
| 639 (b, c) | Fouled from behind on breakaway |

### Awarded Goal

| 406 (b) | Thrown stick during penalty shot |
| 406 (f) | Interference or distraction during penalty shot |
| 621 (f) | Illegal player interference with goalkeeper removed |

# Rules Governing the Game
## of Inline Hockey

## Official Signals

## BOARDING

Striking the closed
fist of the hand once
into the open palm
of the other hand.

## BUTT-ENDING

Moving the forearm,
fist closed, under
the other forearm,
hand held palm
down.

## CHARGING

Rotating clenched
fists around one
another in front of
chest.

## CHECKING FROM BEHIND

Arm placed behind
the back, elbow
bent, forearm paral-
lel to the playing
surface.

## CROSS-CHECKING

A forward motion
with both fists
clenched, extending
from the chest.

## DELAYED CALLING OF PENALTY

The non-whistle
hand is extended
straight above the
head.

## DELAYING THE GAME

The non-whistle hand, palm open, is placed across the chest and then fully extended directly in front of the body.

## ELBOWING

Tapping the elbow with the opposite hand.

## FIGHTING - ROUGHING - BODY CHECKING

One punching
motion to the side
with the arm
extending from the
shoulder.

## GOAL SCORED

A single point, with
the non-whistle
hand, directly at the
goal in which the
puck/ball legally
entered, while
simultaneously
blowing the whistle.

## HAND PASS

The non-whistle hand (open hand) and arm are placed straight down along-side the body and swung forward and up once in an under-hand motion.

## HIGH-STICKING

Holding both fists, clenched, one immediately above the other, at the side of the head.

## HOLDING

Clasping the wrist
of the whistle hand
well in front of the
chest.

## HOLDING THE FACE MASK

Closed fist held in
front of face, palm
in, and pulled down
in one straight
motion.

## HOOKING

A tugging motion
with both arms, as if
pulling something
toward the stomach.

## INTERFERENCE

Crossed arms sta-
tionary in front of
chest with fists
closed.

## KNEEING

A single tap of the
right knee with the
right hand.

## MATCH PENALTY

Pat flat palm of
hand on the top of
the head.

## MISCONDUCT

Placing of both
hands on hips one
time.

## PENALTY SHOT

Arms crossed (fists
clenched) above
head.

## SLASHING

One chop of the
hand across the
straightened forearm
of the other hand.

## SPEARING

A single jabbing
motion with both
hands together,
thrust forward from
in front of the chest,
then dropping hands
to the side.

## TIMEOUT OR UNSPORTSMANLIKE CONDUCT

Using both hands to form a "T."

## TRIPPING

Strike the side of the knee and follow-through once, keeping the head up.

## WASHOUT

Both arms swung laterally across the body at shoulder level with palms down. It means no goal or infraction, so play shall continue.

# Rules Governing the Game
of Inline Hockey

# Rink Diagrams

## InLine Hockey Rink Diagram

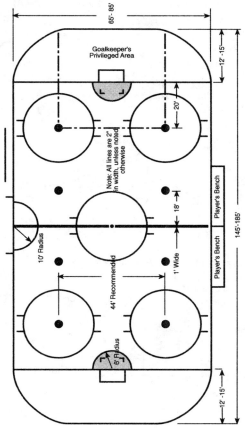

## End Zone Face-Off Circles

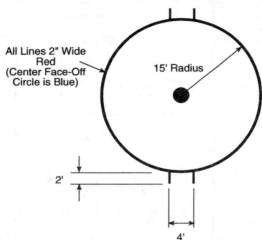

All Lines 2" Wide
Red
(Center Face-Off
Circle is Blue)

15' Radius

2'

4'

## End Zone and Special Face-Off Spots

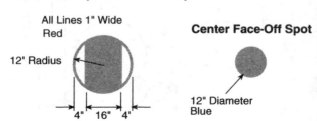

All Lines 1" Wide
Red

12" Radius

4" 16" 4"

### Center Face-Off Spot

12" Diameter
Blue

**Center Red Line**

**Goal Line and Goal Crease**

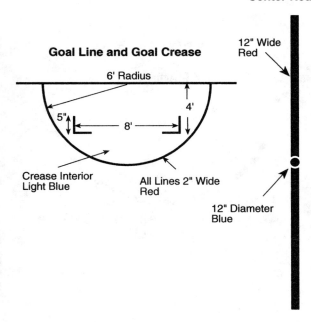

12" Wide
Red

6' Radius

4'

5"

8'

Crease Interior
Light Blue

All Lines 2" Wide
Red

12" Diameter
Blue

**Referee's Crease**

10' Radius

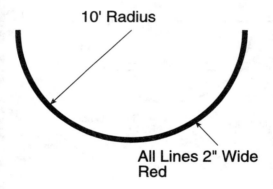

All Lines 2" Wide
Red

# Rules Governing the Game
## of Inline Hockey

# Glossary

## Age Divisions

The following age divisions have been established for all teams registered with USA Hockey InLine.

| Age Divisions | Boys'/Men's | Girls'/Women's |
|---|---|---|
| Mites | 8-and-Under | N/A |
| Squirts | 10-and-Under | 8-12 |
| Pee Wees | 12-and-Under | 13-15 |
| Bantams | 14-and-Under | N/A |
| Midgets | 17-and-Under | 16-19 |
| High School | Enrolled in High School | |
| Adults | 18-and-Over | Any Age |
| College/Club | Enrolled in College | |

*(Note 1) Girls/Women playing on a Boys'/Men's team must conform to the Boys'/ Men's age division.*

*(Note 2) To promote the standardization and consistency of the playing rules between leagues nationwide, sanctioned leagues must utilize the following age determination date(s):*

> *1999-2000 Membership Registration Season - Player's age on December 31, 1999*

> *2000-2001 Membership Registration Season - Player's age on December 31, 2000*

*(Note 3) The USA Hockey InLine Regional and*

---

*National Championships will utilize the following age determination date(s) for the 1999, 2000 and 2001 Championships:*

> *1999 Regional and National Championships - Player's age on December 31, 1998*
>
> *2000 Regional and National Championships - Player's age on December 31, 1999*
>
> *2001 Regional and National Championships - Player's age on December 31, 2000*

*(Note 4) Leagues shall have the option of allowing players to play up one age division, provided such a player's skill level and physical maturity is of similarity to other participants in the age division. Allowing players to play down an age division is prohibited.*

### Altercation

Any physical interaction between two or more opposing players resulting in a penalty or penalties being assessed.

### Break-Away

A condition whereby a player is in control of the puck/ball with no opposition between the player and the opposing goal, with a reasonable scoring opportunity.

### Butt-Ending

The condition whereby a player uses the shaft of the stick above the upper hand to jab or attempt to jab an opposing player.

# Coach

A Coach is a person primarily responsible for directing and guiding the play of the team. Along with the Manager, the Coach is responsible for the conduct of the team's players before, during and after a game.

# Creases

*Goalkeeper's:* Areas marked on the playing surface in front of each goal designed to protect the goalkeepers from interference by attacking players.

*Referee's:* Area marked on the playing surface in front of the Penalty Timekeeper's seat for the use of the Game Officials.

# Cross-Checking

When a player, holding the stick with both hands, checks an opponent by using the shaft of the stick with no part of the stick on the playing surface.

# Deflecting the Puck/Ball

The action of the puck/ball contacting any person or object, causing it to change direction.

# Directing the Puck

The act of intentionally moving or positioning the body, skate or stick so as to change the course of the puck/ball in a desired direction.

# Face-Off

The action of an Official dropping the puck/ball between the sticks of two opposing players to start play. A face-off begins when the Referee indicates its location and the Officials take their appropriate positions and ends when the puck/ball has been legally dropped.

## Fighting

The actual throwing of a punch(es) (closed fist) by a player which makes contact with an opponent.

## Game(s) Suspension

Any player, Coach or Manager who receives a game suspension(s), shall not be eligible to participate in the next game(s) that were already on the schedule of that team before the incident occurs.

## Goalkeeper

A goalkeeper is a person designated as such by a team and is permitted special equipment and privileges to prevent the puck/ball from entering the goal.

## Head-Butting

The physical use of one's head in the course of delivering a body-check (head first) in the chest, head, neck or back area or the physical use of the head to strike an opponent.

## HECC

The Hockey Equipment Certification Council is an independent organization responsible for the development, evaluation and testing of performance standards for protective hockey equipment. Equipment that is approved by HECC is recommended for all players.

## Heel of the Stick

The point where the shaft of the stick and the bottom of the blade meet.

## Hooking

The action of applying the blade of the stick to any part of an opponent's body or stick and impeding the progress by a pulling or tugging motion with the stick.

## League Authorities

The immediate governing body of the team or teams involved, except: In USA Hockey InLine Tournaments and Play-Offs, the body shall be the Discipline Committee of the Tournament or Play-Off.

## Off-Rink Official

Officials appointed to assist in the conduct of the game, including the Official Scorer, Game Timekeeper, Penalty Timekeeper and the two Goal Judges.

## Penalty

A penalty is the result of an infraction of the rules by a player or Team Official. It usually involves the removal from the game of the offending player or Team Official for a specified period of time. In some cases the penalty may be the awarding of a penalty shot on goal or the actual awarding of a goal.

## Player

Member of a team physically participating in a game. The goalkeeper is considered a player except where special rules specify otherwise.

## Possession of the Puck/Ball

The last player or goalkeeper to make contact with the puck/ball. This includes a puck/ball that is deflected off a player or any part of the equipment.

# Possession and Control of the Puck/Ball

The last player or goalkeeper to make contact with the puck/ball and to propel the puck/ball in a desired direction.

# Protective Equipment

Equipment worn by players for the sole purpose of protection from injury. All equipment should be commercially manufactured.

# Shorthanded

Shorthanded means that a team is below the numerical strength of its opponents on the playing surface. Thus, if an equal number of players from each team is each serving a penalty(s) (minor, bench minor, major or match only), neither team is "shorthanded."

# Slashing

The action of striking or attempting to strike an opponent with a stick or swinging a stick at an opponent with no contact being made.

# Spearing

The action of poking or attempting to poke an opponent with the tip of the blade of the stick while holding the stick with one or both hands.

# Substitute Goalkeeper

A designated goalkeeper on the Official Score Sheet who is not participating in the game.

# Team Official

A person responsible in any degree for the operation of a team, such as a Team Executive, Coach, Manager or Trainer.

# Temporary Goalkeeper

A player not designated as a goalkeeper on the Official Score Sheet who assumes that position when no designated goalkeeper is able to participate in the game. The temporary goalkeeper is governed by goalkeeper privileges and limitations, and must return as a "player" when a designated goalkeeper becomes available to participate in the game.

# Index to the
# Rules of
# Inline Hockey